C000100500

AMAZING AND EXTRAORDINARY FACTS

THE
BRITISH AT WAR

AMAZING AND EXTRAORDINARY FACTS

THE
BRITISH AT WAR

Jonathan Bastable

RP

RYDON
PUBLISHING

A Rydon Publishing Book
35 The Quadrant
Hassocks
West Sussex
BN6 8BP

www.rydonpublishing.co.uk
www.rydonpublishing.com

Revised edition first published by Rydon Publishing in 2018
First published by David & Charles in 2011

ISBN: 978-1-910821-23-7

Printed in Poland by BZGraf. SA

CONTENTS

For Alison, with love and thanks

INTRODUCTION

Few nations have a longer warlike tradition than Britain, and none has an army that has fought in more far-flung and fearsome corners of the globe than the British Army. English-speaking soldiers have been pretty much everywhere, and usually there is a military cemetery, large or small, to prove it.

The recorded history of Britain's wars goes back 2,000 years, to Julius Caesar's failed attempt to conquer the island. The successful Roman invasion came a century later, and the only other conquest of Britain by a foreign power (the Normans) more or less exactly a millennium after that – precisely at the halfway point, you might say, of this country's history.

In between the Romans and the Normans the country endured the manifold incursions of the Angles, Saxons, Jutes and Vikings. Their takeover of Britain was too protracted and too piecemeal to be called a conquest; it might better be termed an incremental series of colonisations, supported by the sword and battle-axe. It almost goes without saying that all Britain's wars in that first millennium were fought on British soil, and that they therefore had a profound effect on the nature and makeup of Britain itself. The national character – that complex alloy of Celtic, Germanic, Scandinavian and Continental elements – was forged and tempered in battles and wars waged in our own fields and hedgerows, on our own beaches and in our own backyards.

Over the course of the next millennium, however, Britain's warriors tested their mettle many times against other nations (and at times, against themselves). It was British soldiers and sailors – doing their gruelling and gruesome work – who carved out the largest Empire the world has known. Whatever one may feel about the rights and wrongs of that imperial project, there can be no doubt that it would never have achieved such spectacular results without countless feats of heroism on the part of individual British fighting men.

That same admirable spirit inhabited the tragic young men – 'half the seed of Europe', as the poet Wilfred Owen put it – who fought and died in the mud of blood of Flanders during the First World War; and it was present in the next generation, the millions of Britons that took part in the mighty and entirely righteous struggle against Nazism. It is no less present in the servicemen and servicewomen of our own day, soldiering away in inhospitable landscapes.

In this book you will find some anecdotes about Britain's outstanding military heroes – medal winners and generals such as Nelson and Wellington. But the real heroes of the book are the unremarkable and often anonymous British soldiers – the men of all ranks, all services and all wars – in the many garbs and incarnations that they have adopted down the centuries of battle. Because in the end, the fascination of war lies not in the military hardware and hierarchies, in the roster of regiments or the orders of battle, but in the fact that war makes ordinary people do extraordinary things. It is an amazing fact that the experience of battle tends to rouse good people to feats of arms and heights of bravery that they never knew they had in them.

To acknowledge that fact is not to glorify war or downplay its horrors; it is to celebrate the courageous, resourceful instinct that resides in each one of us, but which the British people choose to believe they possess in special measure – especially when the game seems up, and their aim is true.

Dressed to Kill
The first uniforms of the English army

For much of English martial history, there was no such thing as a military uniform. True, crusaders wore the cross of St George – red on white, and sewn to a sleeve or some other part of the clothing. And the knights of the age of chivalry carried shields bearing a coat of arms that identified them personally. But ordinary soldiers fought and died in their own workaday clothes.

So in the melée of a medieval battle, it would have been hard to tell friend from foe. Friends, perhaps, one would have known personally – or at least by sight, having marched with them. Enemies would have been known by some local and unfamiliar quirk of dress, as well as by the language (or at least the accent) in which they cursed and screamed.

The need for some unmistakable way of distinguishing one's own men became acute with the outbreak of the English Civil War. The political divide between royalists and parliamentarians cut through

geographical and social boundaries, and members of the same family found themselves in opposite camps and opposing armies. We now imagine that all Roundheads sported the same pudding-bowl haircut, and all Royalists were dandified cavaliers in plumed hats. There is some truth in that, but the fact is that there was not always an obvious way to tell the factions apart, at least not on the battlefield. So in the first encounters of the war, beginning in 1642, men of all ranks on both sides took to wearing sashes in distinctive colours.

It was in 1645, with the formation of the New Model Army under Thomas Fairfax, that standardised uniforms first made an appearance. The New Model Army was an elite fighting force consisting of 22,000 men assigned to 11 regiments of horse, 12 infantry regiments, and a 1,000-strong detachment of dragoons (mounted infantry) – all of them dressed in the same red coats. And it was not just their coats that they had in common. Every element of their uniform equipment – shirts, knapsacks, belts – was standardised and centrally sourced, as this detailed order placed with a supplier in London makes clear: 'Two Thousand Coates and Two Thousand Breeches at seventeen shillings a Coat and Breeches... The coates to be of a Red Colour and of Suffolk, Coventry, or Gloucester-Shire Cloth... Three Quarters and Nayle long, according to a pattern delivered... The Breeches to Be of Grey & Made of Reading Cloth... The stockings to be of good Welsh Cotton.' In the course of 1645, the quartermasters of the New Model Army also contracted for 4,500 pairs of shoes 'sevrall sizes of Tennes, Eleavens, Twelves and thirteenes', more than 11,000 guns, 9,000 infantry swords, as well as 'Pikes of good Ash, sixteen Foote long with steele heads at three shillings tenpence a pike' and '2000 Bandoleers to bee of wood with whole bottoms to be turned within and not bored, with good belts... to be brought to the Tower of London immediately...'

The order books make it clear that there was a very efficient machine behind the Roundhead army, which is surely one of the reasons they won in the end. More intangible is the psychological effect of wearing a uniform, which must have been the same for a soldier then as it is for a soldier now. It would have made those New Model Army men feel that they were part of a unit, it would have instilled a sense of pride and purpose, it would have been an outward sign of an all-pervasive military discipline. (The New Model Army were also given regular pay, an entirely new idea that must have done wonders for morale).

And the uniform impressed onlookers – both those who were for the Roundheads and those who were against. The professional air of the army certainly caused a stir in May 1645 when, newly fitted out, they set out from Windsor to lay siege to Oxford: 'The manner of Sir Thomas Fairfaxes march is thus,' wrote one eyewitness. 'Major Skippon marched in the van of the foot and leadeth the Generalls own regiment... the men are Red-coats all the whole army, only are distinguished by the several facings of their coats, the fire-locks only some of them are tauny coates; and thus the regiments of foot march one after the other.'

THE SIGN OF ST GEORGE
The red-and-white cross of St George was the sole identifier of the men who served under Edward Longshanks in his campaigns against the Welsh. Later, it was customary for certain

types of soldier from the same locality to dress in a similar manner. In the 14th century, archers from the county of Cheshire were instantly recognisable on the battlefield because they all wore coats and hats in green and white. Soldiers of Norfolk traditionally wore distinctive white surcoats, which must have made them look like tooled-up lab technicians on an outing to the countryside.

From Rome to Roses
Britain's wars from Julius Caesar to Richard III

Julius Caesar's first invasion of Britain (55BC)

Julius Caesar's second invasion of Britain (54BC)

Claudius' conquest of Britain (43-84AD)

Anglo-Saxon Britain (5th-6th century)

Viking invasions of Britain (793–1066)

The Norman Conquest of England (1066-1088)

The Nineteen-Year Winter (1135–1154)

The Revolt (1173-1174)

The Kings' Crusade (1189-1192, Middle East)

The French Wars (1194-1214)

The Welsh uprising (1211)

The First Barons' War (1215–1217)

The French campaigns of Henry III (1230-1254)

The Second Barons' War (1264–1267)

The Welsh Uprising (1282)

The French War of Edward I (1294-1303)

The First War of Scottish Independence (1296–1328)

Queen Isabella's overthrow of Edward II (1326)

The Second War of Scottish Independence (1332–1357)

The Hundred Years War (1337–1453)

The Wars of the Roses (1455–1485)

Roman Enemy at the Gates
Julius Caesar lands in Britain

Julius Caesar twice attempted to subdue the strange triangular island of the coast of Gaul, and twice failed. His first attempt to conquer Britain took place in 55BC. He embarked from Boulogne with 12,000 troops in ships designed for the still waters of the Mediterranean. They were not well suited to the stormy, tidal waters of the Channel, and it made for an uncomfortable crossing. When his fleet came close to English coast he saw that Britons were waiting for him. They were gathered on the white cliffs near Dover, ready to throw spears down on the heads of the Romans when they tried to land. Caesar was too good a general to let that happen, so he sailed up the coast to a point near Walmer, and began to disembark with his army.

'But the [British] barbarians saw what we were planning,' Caesar later wrote, 'and sent forward their horsemen and charioteers (their favourite form of attack), and as the rest of their forces followed they attempted to prevent our men landing. Our ships, on account of their size, could be stationed only in deep water; and our soldiers, not knowing the lie of the land, with their hands encumbered, weighed down with heavy armour, had to leap from the ships, stand in the surf, and face up to the enemy. The Britons, on the other hand, were either on dry ground, or advancing a little way into the water. Their hands were free, and they knew where the shallows were. They could confidently throw their weapons and spur on their horses, which were accustomed to this kind of service. Dismayed by these circumstances and altogether untrained in this mode of battle, our men did not all exert the same vigour and eagerness which they had been wont to exert in engagements on dry ground.'

It was only an individual act of valour that saved the landings from total failure. 'While our men were hesitating on account of the depth of the sea, the standard-bearer of the tenth legion exclaimed, "Jump, men, unless you want to lose your eagle to the enemy. I, for my part, will perform my duty to the commonwealth and my general." He then leaped from the ship and proceeded to carry the eagle toward the enemy. Then our men all leaped from the ship to save themselves from disgrace. When those in the other ships saw them, they charged the enemy too.'

The Romans reached land, but that was not the end of their difficulties. Those British chariots – ancient prototypes of a much later British invention, the ironclad tank – were particularly troublesome. They were

a tactical weapon that the legionaries were not used to, and so had no sure means of countering.

'Their manner of fighting with chariots is this,' wrote Caesar. 'Firstly, they drive about in all directions and throw their weapons and generally break the ranks of the enemy with the very dread of their horses and the noise of their wheels. And when they have worked themselves in between the troops of horse, they leap from their chariots and engage on foot. The charioteers in the meantime withdraw some little distance from the battle, and so place themselves with the chariots that, if their masters are overpowered by the number of the enemy, they may have a ready retreat to their own troops. Thus they display in battle the speed of cavalry and the steadfastness of infantry.'

Caesar had left it until late in the summer to launch his invasion, and it rapidly became clear to him that he was unlikely to gain a foothold in Britain before the winter came. Rather than sit in enemy territory and wait to be starved out, he retreated back over the water with nothing much to show for the invasion apart from a handful of hostages. He returned the following year and established a bridgehead, and even made some local allies, but never succeeded in subduing the painted warlike Britons on the south coast.

Nearly 90 years later, the insane emperor Caligula planned to invade Britain and so show that he could triumph where Caesar failed, but his troops never got further than the French side of the Channel. Here, in full battle array, the legionaries were commanded to collect seashells in their helmets and tunics. Caligula took the shells back to Rome as 'plunder from the ocean'.

Quite what Caligula meant by turning the planned invasion of Britain into a silly seaside farce is not known. Possibly he lost his nerve and – in his madness – exacted tribute from the sea-god Neptune instead of from the Britons. Or it might be that the emperor's superstitious troops refused to go to the ghost-ridden, fog-laden white island across the sea, and Caligula forced them to gather worthless shells as an ironic comment on their lack of courage. At any rate, the Roman conquest of Britain had

to wait a few more years – until the reign of Caligula's uncle and successor, Claudius the First.

Vees–up for Victory
England's warlike two-fingered salute

The V-sign is a quintessentially British gesture, and also a strangely ambiguous one. When the

index and middle finger are flicked up with the palm outwards, it signifies victory, or the hope of it. The same gesture with the palm inwards is an obscene visual message meaning – to put it mildly – 'Get lost'. Both signs, with their different meanings, are bound up in England's wars with her enemies.

The insulting palm-inward V-sign is said to date back to the Battle of Agincourt. According to the story, the French let it be known before the battle that any English archers taken prisoner would have their bowstring fingers cut off – so that they would never be able to fire arrows at Frenchmen again. At the end of the battle, the English archers taunted the defeated French by displaying their two fingers intact – and herein lies the origin of the gesture.

But the story may not be true, or not entirely. There is no documentary evidence that the French ever planned to mutilate English archers in that way. There were certainly no French documents suggesting that such an order was given (despite what authorities have claimed). But a French chronicler named Jean de

Waurin, who fought at Agincourt, says that King Henry, speaking to his archers on the eve of battle, told them that the French would 'cut off three fingers of the right hand' if they caught them alive. Whether Henry knew that to be true, or was just disseminating anti-French propaganda to make his troops fight all the harder, is impossible to know. But the fact that de Waurin mentions three fingers makes it seem less likely that Agincourt is the source of the two-fingered salute. It is more probable that the gesture goes back much further in time. It may well be a slightly elaborated phallic gesture, like the raised middle finger used in Mediterranean lands (and later in the USA), or the Slavonic *kukish*, in which the thumb is inserted between the first two fingers of the same hand and raised as a fist.

Whatever its origin, the British 'vees-up' was in common use by the lower classes in Victorian times and in the early part of the 20th century. The palm-outward victory sign seems to have been unknown until Winston Churchill popularised it in the Second World War. Clearly it is intended to suggest the 22nd letter of the alphabet, and it may be Churchill's own invention.

Early on in the war, the prime minister seems to have been happy to make the sign either way round, indiscriminately. He was of aristocratic stock, and clearly did not know that the orientation of the hand made a significant difference to the working-class population. Presumably someone had a word in his ear, because by the end of the war a 'V for victory' salute was always displayed palm-out. There is a photograph of Churchill doing the V to a line of factory workers at some point in the middle of the war. Interestingly, all the workers in front of him are signalling victory to his face, while all the workers located behind his back are sending him a less flattering message, palms inwards.

The distinction still remains, in Britain at least. But in the 1960s, the victory sign acquired a new layer of meaning when it began to be used by hippies throughout the English-speaking world to signify 'peace'. Most likely, this came about because peace – in the sense of a cessation of hostilities – is a natural consequence of victory. But it is nonetheless strange that a gesture steeped in war and vengeance has, to later generations, come to stand for an ideal of pacifism and universal brotherhood.

Full Metal Jacket
An English knight and his armour

The suit of armour that we think of as the standard battledress of an English knight was slow to evolve. Over the course of four centuries

finely wrought metal pieces – which were tailored and shaped to the bodies of individual knights – ousted the chainmail suits that were worn by the men of William the Conqueror's Norman army.

In the 15th century the full suit of plate armour reached a level of technological and aesthetic perfection. A fully kitted-out knight of that era would ride into battle wearing an elaborate helmet (the great helm), which might feature a crest and other partly decorative features such as a snout-shaped visor. His chest would be protected by a breastplate (a piece of protective kit borrowed from the sporting joust) worn over a quilted jacket known as a *gambeson* or an *aketon*. This would be fixed to a backplate, so as to entirely encase the torso.

He would wear *brassarts* on his upper arms, *gauntlets* on his hands, *poleyns* on his thighs, *greaves* on his shins, and jointed *sabatons* on his feet, like a pair of metal slippers. At his elbows he might have leather pads, or else an elaborately fanned joint that offered complete protection while still allowing enough freedom

of movement to wield a sword or a lance. A knight's horse would have armour of its own – a chainmail skirt known as a 'trapper', and a plate to protect its head and nose – called a *chanfron*. The mounts themselves were huge sturdy beasts, more like shire horses than the sleek, slim thoroughbreds ridden by modern-day cavalry regiments.

Naturally, a suit of armour had to be made by a master craftsman, and the best armourers in Europe were to be found in Milan, or else in various cities in Germany. Henry VIII had several suits of German-made armour, most of them intended to be worn on sporting occasions rather than in war, as by his time the age of the full suit of armour was drawing to a close.

One of Henry's suits weighs 94 pounds (43 kilogrammes) so it is no surprise that he sometimes had to be winched onto his horse. He did once wear his armour in battle, at the siege of Boulogne in 1544. The suit in question had been made four years earlier; in the interim, his legs had swollen due to a chronic abscess, and part of the armour had to be cut away so that he could fit into it.

'Vain and Silly…'
When Wellington met Nelson

The Duke of Wellington and Lord Nelson are sometimes seen as mirror images of each other – Britain's two outstanding war-leaders of the Napoleonic era, one on land, the other at sea. In terms of character and personality, too, they could hardly have been more different. Wellington was gruff, plain-speaking, unpretentious; Nelson, his immense personal courage notwithstanding, was vain, self-conscious, and inordinately fond of the awards and titles that were showered on him.

The meeting between these two giants of British military history came about completely by chance, in London on September 10th, 1805. Nelson by that time was a long-standing national hero, at home for a few weeks before putting out to sea; Wellington was a successful but still little-known commander, recently returned from a long campaign against the Maratha Empire in India. It was a strange encounter:

'I went to the Colonial Office in Downing Street,' wrote Wellington, 'and there I was shown into the little waiting room on the right-hand side where I found, also waiting to see the Secretary of State, a gentleman whom, from his likeness to his pictures and the loss of an arm, I immediately recognised as Lord Nelson. He could not know who I was, but he entered at once into conversation with me, if I can call it conversation, for it was almost all on his side and all about himself, and in, really, a style so vain and silly as to surprise and almost disgust me.

'I suppose something that I happened to say may have made him guess that I was *somebody*, and he went out of the room for a moment, I have no doubt to ask the office-keeper who I was, for when he came back he was altogether a different man, both in manner and matter. All that I had thought a charlatan style had vanished, and he talked of the state of this country, and of the aspect and probabilities of affairs on the Continent with a good sense, and a knowledge of subjects both at home and abroad that surprised me… in fact he talked like an officer and a statesman.

'The Secretary of State kept us long waiting, and certainly, for the last half or three-quarters of an hour, I don't know that I ever had a conversation that interested me more. Now, if the Secretary of State had been punctual, and admitted Lord Nelson in the first quarter of an hour, I should have had the same impression of a light and trivial character that other people have had.'

That first encounter between Wellington and Nelson was also their last. Within a few weeks, Nelson was dead – shot by a French sniper at the Battle of Trafalgar.

Resisting Rome
Boudicca's war against the invading legions

After almost a century of trying, Rome finally launched a successful invasion of Britain in 43AD. The attacking force consisted of 40,000 men – more than three times more than Julius Caesar's army of 55BC – and it was too strong for the native Britons to resist. The legions landed in Kent and rapidly

spread inland, conquering tribe after tribe and turning local leaders into compliant client kings.

But all that progress stalled – in fact, the Roman conquest of Britain almost came to an ignominious end – when the legions came up against Boudicca, queen of the Iceni.

The Iceni were a Celtic tribe that occupied what is now Norfolk. Their leader, Prasutagus, quickly reached an accommodation with the Romans when they arrived, and his people were left more or less in peace. But he died in 60AD, leaving his lands equally to the Emperor Nero and to his two daughters.

This in effect made a queen of the girls' mother, Boudicca, which created a problem for the Romans, because Imperial law prohibited female inheritance. So the occupying army marched into Iceni territory to impose its own rules on the Iceni. The Romans behaved in the most brutal way. They sacked Prasutagus' palace as if he had been an enemy rather than a vassal. According to some accounts Boudicca was flogged, and her daughters raped.

The intention had been to cow Boudicca and her people, but the gross maltreatment meted out by the legionaries backfired spectacularly. It sparked a bloody revolt that was led by the furious Boudicca herself. 'In stature she was very tall,' wrote the Roman historian Dio Cassius, 'In appearance most terrifying, in the glance of her eye most fierce, and her voice was harsh; a great mass of the tawniest hair fell to her hips…'

Boudicca gathered an army from the ranks of her own people and swept south into core Roman territory, rallying other disaffected tribes as she went. Her confederation of Celtic Britons put the town of Camulodunum (Colchester) to the torch, then descended on Londinium (London). Here the Roman population was butchered in ways at least as cruel as the soldiers of Rome had meted out to Boudicca and her family. The Celtic army then rolled on to Verulamium (St Albans) and burned that town to the ground too.

'The barbarians enjoyed plundering and thought of nothing else,' wrote Tacitus, the other Roman historian of the revolt. 'They ignored forts and garrisons, and instead made for where loot was richest and protection weakest. Roman and provincial deaths at the places mentioned are estimated at seventy thousand. For the British did not take or sell prisoners, or practise war-time exchanges. They could not wait to cut throats, hang, burn, and crucify – as though avenging in advance the retribution that was on its way.'

Boudicca's rapid progress was due in part to the fact that a large part of the Roman army was absent, waging war against the druids of Anglesey. Their commander, Suetonius Paulinus, was in Wales with his army. As soon as he received news of the carnage in the south-east, he marched back with three legions. Boudicca meanwhile had swung north-west, and the two armies met on the long highway known as Watling Street, somewhere in the west Midlands.

The most likely site for the battle that then ensued is the Roman fort at Manduessedum (modern-day Mancetter, in Warwickshire). Here, Boudicca's confederation was decisively defeated, and the rebellion came to an end. But back in Rome, the Emperor Nero was so shaken by the events in Britain that he considered abandoning the island altogether. How different British history might have been had he acted on that thought, and Roman rule had endured not for almost 400 years, but for less than 20.

As for Boudicca, she died on the day of the battle – possibly by her own hand. Her legend lives on. She was idealised by the Victorians (who misnamed her Boadicea), and she has become partly conflated with the metaphorical figure of Britannia, the female embodiment of British nationhood. A grand bronze statue of her stands by the Thames in Westminster, in the heart of the city that she merrily destroyed. There is a long-standing tradition – entirely fictitious – that she is buried beneath Platform 10 at King's Cross Station.

HADRIAN'S FOLLY

The Roman invasion of Britain was never completed. The aim of Emperor Claudius, when he dispatched his legions, was always to subjugate all of the British mainland, the territory we now think of as England, Scotland and Wales. That never happened, because no Roman general ever managed to stabilise the northern border. Hadrian's wall, which marks the northernmost frontier of the Roman Empire, is in some ways a monument to the Romans' military failure.

Sergeant-Major Gandhi
A great soul in the British Army

Mohandas Gandhi, the prophet of non-violence and architect of Indian independence, twice served in the British armed forces. In 1899, when the Boer War broke out, Gandhi was working in Natal as a lawyer. He felt that it might help Indians in South Africa to win civil rights if they were seen to take on civic responsibilities, such as serving in the army. It was with this in mind that he raised an Indian Ambulance Corps consisting of more than 1,000 men. Gandhi, along with several dozen other Indian servicemen, was awarded the War Medal.

Seven years later, in 1906, he tried to persuade the authorities to allow Indians to fight against the rebellious Zulus. The British refused to put Indians under arms, but allowed them to work as stretcher-bearers under the command of Gandhi, who held the rank of sergeant-major. This experience was rather more equivocal for Gandhi, and seems to have reinforced his commitment to non-violence: 'The Boer War had not

brought home to me the horrors of war with anything like the vividness that the "rebellion" did. This was no war but a man-hunt, not only in my opinion, but also in that of many Englishmen with whom I had occasion to talk.' He still felt it was acceptable to help those wounded in battle, however. When the Great War broke out in 1914 Gandhi, now in England, helped recruit a Field Ambulance Corps from among Indian students living in London.

THE FIRST ENGLISH VICTORY

The Battle of Ashdown, fought on January 8th in the year 871, can be said to be the first victory of English arms. The clash was between an army of Danes and a slightly larger force of a West Saxons – perhaps 1,000 men – led by a 21-year-old prince who would later be known to history as Alfred the Great. Alfred had summoned his army from a place called Blowingstone Hill on

AELFREDUS
MAGNUS

Ex ... ...

the Berkshire Downs. On top of the hill was an ancient standing stone with a hole in it. By blowing in the hole in the right way, it was said, the stone could be made to sound like a trumpet. This is what Alfred did, and legend says that all the fighting men within earshot rallied to his side.

The two armies met at a place called Compton (the name of which could be taken to mean 'place of

conflict'), where there stood a lone thorn tree. There was a great clash of shield walls that resulted in the Danes being forced back, like the weaker side in a rugby scrum. The Danish line collapsed, and their army fled eastwards, pursued by the English. It was said that Danish corpses were strewn across the Downs like fallen leaves – hundreds of them, all the way to Reading.

The Rough Wooing and Other Wars
Britain's conflicts from 1494 to 1713

The Habsburg–Valois Wars (1494–1559, Italy and southern Europe)

The Cornish Rebellion (1497, southern England)

The Scottish Wars (1513–1523)

The War of the Rough Wooing (1544–1551, Scotland)

The Prayerbook Rebellion (1549, Cornwall and Devon)

The Desmond Rebellions
(1569-1583, Ireland)

The Spanish Wars
(1585-1604)

The Spanish Armada (1588)

Tyrone's Rebellion
(1594–1603, Ireland)

The Dutch War of Independence
(1598–1648)

The First and Second Powhatan Wars (1609–1622, America)

The Anglo-French War
(1626-1629)

The Bishops' Wars
(1639-40, Scotland)

The Irish Rebellion and Confederate War (1641-48)

The English Civil War
(1642–1651)

Cromwell's conquest of Ireland
(1649-1653)

The Third Anglo-Powhatan War
(1644)

The First Anglo-Dutch War
(1652–1654)

The Anglo-Spanish War
(1654–1660)

The Second Anglo-Dutch War
(1665–1667)

The French Revenge War
(1667–1668)

The Third Anglo-Dutch War
(1672–1674)

Metacom's War
(1675–1676, North America)

Bacon's Rebellion (1676, Virginia)

The Monmouth Rebellion
(1685, the west of England)

The War of the Grand Alliance
(1688–1697, Europe, North America)

The Williamite War
(1689-1691, Ireland)

Our Murderous Scallywags
The would-be guerrillas of Nazi Britain

Since the British Isles have rarely been occupied by an invader, the history of Britain at war contains only a handful of resistance fighters or guerrilla episodes. There is Boudicca's almost-successful revolt against the legions in the early days of Roman rule, and there is the rather more

uncertain trail of mayhem left by Hereward the Wake in his one-man campaign against the Normans. And had Hitler succeeded in landing on British soil in 1940, there would have been the bizarre but glorious actions of the Scallywags.

The Scallywags were a secret network of saboteurs and assassins set up in Britain after the retreat from Dunkirk. The detachments who made this fighting force were officially known as GHQ Auxiliary Units, and they were drawn from the ranks of men who had local knowledge, and usually some past military experience, but were generally too old to enlist. They also had to be unlikely-looking candidates: among their ranks were farmers, vicars, medical men, accountants. The parliamentarian and future Labour leader Michael Foot is said to have been a scallywag, as are the writers JP Priestley and George Orwell.

In total there were about 6,000 scallywags, all of them assigned to local Home Guard units as a kind of relatively innocuous cover. They operated in groups of six or seven, having received brief but intense training in the summer months of 1940. Each undercover scallywag carried a note – a Get Out of Jail Free card – to be produced if they were picked up by the loyal British authorities. It asked any copper who collared a gent acting suspiciously – carrying a gun, say – to 'ask no questions of the bearer but phone this number'.

The scallywags had a motto of their own, 'Terror By Night'; and if the Germans had invaded much of their work would have been terrible and

nocturnal. They were ready to blow up railway lines, take on the Nazi war machine, and even assassinate collaborators (including any members of a puppet Nazi parliament). Their jocular term for the work they were trained for was 'scallywagging', hence their informal name.

The tools for the job – wads of money, caches of weapons and explosives – were issued in advance and carefully hidden in the English countryside. Each unit was also supplied with a gallon of rum. It was thought that a tot or two might help them resist interrogation if caught by the Gestapo.

That did not come to pass – no German SS-man or secret policeman ever set foot on British soil – and the official issue of rum was no doubt put to more congenial uses. But though the services of the scallywags were never required, their intent was real and deadly serious. There is every reason to believe that, had it come to it, they would have acquitted themselves with every bit as much ruthlessness and valour as the gallant French *maquis* or the fearsome partisans of the Russian forests.

The Whites of their Eyes
The secret of close-order firing

The expression 'Don't fire till you can see the whites of their eyes' has become a kind of military cliché – a strange evocation of the close-order firing method used by British colonial armies all over the Empire.

Some sources say that the order was first given at the Battle of Bunker Hill in 1775, but it is not clear which commander said it. Whoever it was, he may have been quoting James Wolfe, who certainly said something along these lines on the Plains of Abraham in 1759. And Wolfe himself was probably repeating a remark made by a German prince, sometimes quoted in lives of Frederick the Great (with which Wolfe would surely have been familiar).

But the earliest definitely attributed use of the phrase belongs to a Scottish officer, the magnificently named Lieutenant-Colonel Sir Andrew Agnew of Lochnaw. At the Battle of Dettingen, which was fought in Bavaria on June 27th, 1743, he gave this order to his Scots Fusiliers as the

French cavalry advanced to engage them: 'Dinna fire till ye can see the whites of their e'en… if ye dinna kill them they'll kill you.' Crucially, of course, the closer the enemy at the moment of firing, the more of them were likely to be hit and killed. The key thing was for the riflemen to hold their nerve.

The French marshall Thomas Bugeaud, who fought against Britain as a junior officer in the Peninsular War, has left an account of what it felt like to face a well-drilled infantry regiment, firing in volleys at close range. As his column advanced towards the British, wrote Bugeaud: 'Some men hoisted their shakos on their musket, the quick-step became a run; the ranks began to be mixed up; the men's agitation became tumultuous, many soldiers began to fire as they ran. And all the while the red English line, still silent and motionless, even when we were only 300 yards away, seemed to take no notice of the storm which was about to break on it.

'At this moment of painful expectation the English line would make a quarter-turn – the muskets

were going up at the "ready".
An indefinable sensation nailed
to the spot many of our men,
who halted and began to open a
wavering fire. The enemy's return,
a volley of simultaneous precision
and deadly effect, crashed upon us
like a thunderbolt. Decimated by
it we reeled together. Then three
formidable *hurrahs*! terminated the
long silence of our adversaries. With
the third they were down upon us,
pressing us into disorderly retreat…'

The Christmas Truce
When the guns stopped for a day

The Christmas truce of 1914,
in the first winter of the Great
War, is often seen today as a parable
of the futility of war – and the ironies
of that one day's peace were not lost
on those who took part. On that
day, in many parts of the Western
Front, German and British troops
spontaneously stopped fighting for
a short while. Instead they left their
trenches and greeted each other,
tentatively, as friends.

There are many accounts of the
truce, and most seem to agree that
the Germans instigated it. It began
on Christmas Eve – which is when
the festivities get under way in the
German tradition. 'The Germans
entrenched opposite us began calling
out to us "Cigarettes", "Pudding",
"A Happy Christmas" and "English
means good",' wrote one English
rifleman named CH Brazier. 'So
two of our fellows climbed over
the parapet of the trench and went
towards the German trenches. Halfway they were met by four Germans,
who said they would not shoot on
Christmas Day if we did not. They
gave our fellows cigars and a bottle
of wine and were given a cake and
cigarettes. When they came back
I went out with some more of our
fellows and we were met by about
30 Germans, who seemed to be very

nice fellows. All through the night we sang carols to them and they sang to us and one played *God Save the King* on a mouth organ.'

Something similar happened further down the front line, near Armentieres. The British troops saw that the Germans, a few hundred yards away, were decorating the lip of their trench with Chinese lanterns. Two British officers went out across no-man's-land and persuaded the first German sentry they encountered to call for an officer of his own. A local ceasefire was agreed for Christmas Day, which was marked with a game of football and an exchange of cigarettes. Football was not everywhere a possibility, because the ground was too churned up, and too thickly sown with corpses, as Rifleman Brazier recounts:

'On Christmas Day we all got out of the trenches and walked about with the Germans, who, when asked if they were fed up with the war, said "Yes, rather". They all believed that London had been captured, and that German sentries were outside Buckingham Palace. They were evidently told a lot of rot. Some of

them could speak English fairly well. Between the trenches there were a lot of dead Germans whom we helped to bury. In one place where the trenches are only 25 yards apart we could see dead Germans half-buried, their legs and gloved hands sticking out of the ground. The trenches in this position are so close that they are called "the Death Trap", as hundreds have been killed there.'

A Private Frederick Heath delighted the Germans in his sector with a present of plum pudding. His rueful joke, that this might be the secret to ending the war, is made, one feels, only half in jest. 'Here was no desire to kill, but just the wish of a few simple soldiers (and no one is quite so simple as a soldier) that on Christmas Day, at any rate, the force of fire should cease. We wrote our names and addresses on the field service postcards, and exchanged them for German ones. We cut the buttons off our coats and took in exchange the Imperial Arms of Germany. But the gift of gifts was Christmas pudding. The sight of it made the Germans' eyes grow wide with hungry wonder, and at the first bite of it they were our friends for ever. Given a sufficient quantity of Christmas puddings, every German in the trenches would have surrendered'.

Heath ended his account, written soon after Christmas, by saying: 'As I finish this short and scrappy description of a strangely human event, we are pouring rapid fire into the German trenches, and they are returning the compliment just as fiercely. Screeching through the air above us are the shattering shells of rival batteries of artillery. So we are back once more to the ordeal of fire.'

Peace broke out again the following Christmas, 1915. 'We could hear "Merry Christmas, Tommy",' wrote Llewellyn Wyn Griffith, an officer in the Royal Welch Fusiliers. We saw hands and bottles being waved at us, with encouraging shouts that we could neither understand nor misunderstand… in a few moments there was a rush of men from both sides, carrying tins of meat, biscuits and other odd commodities for barter.' An afternoon football match was mooted, but this time the senior command was wise to what was going on up at the front. A brigadier

'came spluttering up to the line' and threatened everybody with courts martial. He ordered an especially intense bombardment of the German positions for that night. Many soldiers on both sides aimed high that Christmas night – they had to fight, but they could avoid killing. But the truce was over. Griffith read in the papers a few days later that there had been no fraternising with the enemy at Christmas because 'hate was too bitter to permit of such a yielding'.

KICK-OFF ON THE SOMME

Footballs made a later, more sinister appearance in the muddy no-man's-land of Flanders. On the eve of the battle of the Somme, an officer named

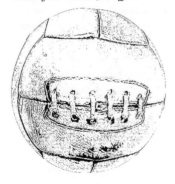

Captain WP Nevill, commander of B Company of the 8th Battalion of the East Surrey Regiment, presented a new football to each of his four platoons, saying that the first to kick its ball all the way to the German trenches would have a prize. One of the platoons found time that evening to paint an inscription on their ball:

> *The Great European Cup*
> *The Final*
> *East Surreys v. Bavarians*
> *Kick-off at Zero*

When zero hour came, on the morning of July 1st, 1916, someone lofted one of the footballs towards the German lines and the East Surreys went over the top, racing into the oncoming machine-gun fire. The regiment lost 147 men that day, and 279 East Surreys were wounded. The 8th Battalion was one of the few to reach its objective – but Nevill's men could not collect their prize: their captain was one of the day's dead. One of the fatal footballs is still to be seen in the museum of the Queen's Royal Surrey Regiment (as it now is) at Clandon Park near Guildford.

Revolts to Revolutions
Britain's wars in the 18th century

Queen Anne's War
(1702–1713, North America)

The First Jacobite Rising
(1715-16, Scotland)

The War of the Quadruple Alliance
(1718–1720)

The War of Jenkins's Ear
(1739–1742)

The War of the Austrian Succession
(1742-48)

The Second Jacobite Rising
(1745-6)

The Seven Years' War
(1756–1763)

The First Mysore War
(1766–1769, India)

The American Revolution
(1775–1783)

The First Maratha War
(1775–1782, India)

The Fourth Dutch War
(1780–1784)

The Second Mysore War
(1780–1784)

The Third Mysore War
(1789–1792)

The French Revolutionary Wars
(1793–1802)

The Fourth Mysore War
(1798–1799, India)

The United Irishmen Rebellion
(1798)

England's Last Battle
A historic exchange of fire on Graveney Marsh

It is generally held that the last pitched battle to be fought on British soil was Culloden, in 1746. In fact, British troops took up arms against a foreign invader much more recently than that, and much further

south. The last battle to be fought on the mainland was a skirmish between the 1st Battalion of the London Irish Rifles and the crew of a downed German aeroplane. It took place on Graveney Marsh, in Kent, on the night of September 27th, 1940.

The Battle of Graveney Marsh is significant for more than its bookend position in British history. It was also an important intelligence coup for the RAF in the early days of the Blitz. It was known that the Germans were flying a new variant of the Junkers 88, and orders had been issued to RAF fighter pilots to capture one intact if possible. The opportunity presented itself on that night. Spitfires and Hurricanes from the 66th and 92nd squadrons spotted one of the new planes on its way back from a raid over London. It was limping along one engine, the other having

been damaged by anti-aircraft fire. The fighters contrived to shoot up its second engine, and the German pilot – Unteroffizier Fritz Ruhlandt – was forced to take his aircraft down onto enemy soil.

Though he was wounded, Ruhlandt managed to make a successful crash-landing on the flat expanse of Graveney Marsh. His Junkers 88 came to a stop a few hundred yards from the Sportsman pub, where the 1st battalion of the London Irish Rifles were billeted.

Soldiers from the battalion were already rushing out of the building, guns in hand, ready to place the Luftwaffe crew under arrest. To their

amazement, the Germans did not surrender; instead the four Germans opened fire with machine-guns. Ruhlandt knew what his aircraft was worth to the British, and he was not about to surrender it without a fight. The British soldiers threw themselves to the ground and returned fire. A group crawled to a dyke a short way away, and began to shoot from there. The Germans, under attack from two directions, gave up the fight and surrendered. No-one had been killed, but one of the Germans was hit in the foot.

Ruhlandt and his crew were taken prisoner. The Irish rifles also took possession of the aircraft, and even removed a time-bomb that had been attached to the plane specifically to prevent its being taken intact.

That ought to have been the end of the incident – but the officer commanding the British detachment, who spoke German, overheard one of the Luftwaffe crew mention that a second device would surely explode at any moment. The officer's name was Captain Cantopher. He now rushed back to the aircraft, found the bomb, and defused it in the nick of time. He was later awarded the George Medal for this act of bravery, which saved the day's prize. When the plane was examined, it turned out to be equipped with a new and sophisticated bombsight.

As for Ruhlandt and his men, they were marched back to the public bar at The Sportsman, where their captors were gracious enough to stand them a few beers before packing them off to a POW camp.

Latham of the Buffs
Defending the colour at the Battle of Albuera

Traditionally, British soldiers have always been fiercely loyal to their own regiments, and the symbol of the regiment is the regimental colour. Nothing could be more disgraceful than to allow the enemy to capture the colour, and there have been occasions when men have performed astonishing acts of courage to hang on to it.

One such incident occurred on May 16th, 1811 at the battle of Albuera, one of the most vicious engagements of the Peninsular War.

The 3rd Regiment of Foot (known as 'the Buffs') had been decimated by Polish lancers, who had incensed their English enemy by spearing the wounded where they lay on the earth. The Poles were about to seize the colours of the 66th when they were snatched from the ground by an English lieutenant.

His name was Matthew Latham. He fought back at the Poles with his sword and was wounded several times, but refused to give let go of the colour on its staff. A French cavalryman made a grab at the flagpole and, rising in his stirrup, landed a swingeing sword blow on Latham's head that severed his nose

and one side of his face. A second hussar brought his sword down on the Latham's left arm, the one that was holding onto the colour, and chopped it off completely. Latham somehow managed to keep a grip on the colour with his right hand, but only by dropping his sword. He sunk to the ground, but tore the silk flag from its staff as he went down. He lay on top of it, and tried to stuff it into his jacket, as the horses of the French and Polish cavalrymen trampled his body and speared him in the back with their lances.

The French did not in the end take the colour from Latham. After the battle was over, it was recovered from his body, and sent to the rear. But Lieutenant Latham – despite appearances and all probability – was not quite dead. Some time after the colour was retrieved he regained consciousness. Unaided, he crawled to a stream, where he was found by some medical orderlies who took him to a convent where his appalling wounds were treated.

As soon as Latham was well enough he was sent back to England. In 1815 he was presented to the Prince Regent at Brighton. The king was so impressed with the story that he paid for a well-known surgeon – a Mr Carpue – to do what he could to repair the terrible damage done at Albuera to Matthew Latham's face.

THE WHIFF OF WAR

It has been said that crusading armies could never mount a successful ambush, at least not if they were upwind of their enemy. They were so foul-smelling that any army could detect their approach with their noses long before they were seen or heard.

The British Soldier...
... as described by his superior officers and others

All through history, for good or ill, generals and field marshalls have felt compelled to express opinions on the quality of their fighting men. Here are some the things that British commanders, enemy commanders, and a few non-combatants on the sidelines have said about the Tommy, his superior officers, and his predecessors.

I don't know what effect these men will have on the enemy, but by God, they terrify me.
The Duke of Wellington
(attributed), 1809

★

As the beast of old must have one young human life as a tribute each year, so to our Empire we throw from day to day the pick and flower of our youth. The engine is worldwide and strong, but the only fuel that will drive it is the lives of British men. If every man had his obelisk, even where he lay, then no frontier line need be drawn, for a cordon of British graves would ever show how high the Anglo-Saxon tide had lapped.

Arthur Conan Doyle

★

The scum of the earth, the mere scum of the earth. It is wonderful that we should be able to make so much of them afterwards. People talk of their enlisting from their fine military

feeling – all stuff, no such thing.
Some of our men enlist from having
got bastard children, some for minor
offences, many more for drink.

The Duke of Wellington, 1811

★

I had rather have a plain russet-coated
captain that knows what he fights for
and loves what he knows, than that
which you call a 'gentleman' and is
nothing else.

Oliver Cromwell, 1643

★

The British infantry are the best in
the world. Fortunately, there are not
many of them.

*Thomas Bugeaud, officer serving under
Napoleon, 1815*

★

I suppose one day the British soldier
will be treated with humanity by his
officers and his country. I hope so. He
is, for all his faults, a noble creature.

Lord Raglan, 1855

★

When the military man approaches,
the world locks up its spoons and
packs off its womankind.

George Bernard Shaw, 1907

★

Have particular attention to that part
of the line which will bear the first
shock of the English troops.

*Louis XIV, advising Marshall Villeroy
before the Battle of Ramillies*

★

[The British soldier has] an
extraordinary bravery and toughness
combined with a rigid inability to
move quickly.

General Erwin Rommel

★

The British soldier can stand
up to anything except the British
War Office.

George Bernard Shaw

★

I am grateful to the British soldiers
– to those small humble citizens
who are capable of being the greatest

soldiers. They do not talk about their deeds; they do not boast; and as soon as the war ends they will modestly disappear into their homes and cease to be heroes. Therein lies their greatest glory.

Jan Masaryk, Czech foreign minister in exile (1886-1948)

★

The tragedy of the Somme was that the best soldiers, the stout-hearted men were lost; their numbers were replaceable, their spiritual worth could never be.

Lord Moran (Churchill's doctor, and veteran of the First World War)

★

I consider nothing in this country so valuable as the life and health of the British soldier.

The Duke of Wellington

★

The pious Greek, when he had set up altars to all the great gods by name, added one more altar 'to the unknown god'. So whenever we speak and think of the great captains and set up our military altars to Hannibal and Napoleon and Marlborough and such like, let us add one more altar 'to the unknown

leader' – that is, to the good company, platoon or section leader who carries forward his men or holds his post, and often falls unknown. It is these who in the end do most to win wars.

Field Marshall The Earl Wavell, 1948

★

TWISTED RICHARD

Richard III may not have been the hunchbacked monster that Shakespeare made him out to be, but he was certainly not what you would call a nice man. On the morning of the Battle of Bosworth, August 22nd, 1485, he emerged from his tent early and happened upon a sentry who had nodded off at his post. Richard stabbed the man as he slept, saying: 'I found him asleep, and have left him as I found him.

Whose Blanket?
Abercromby and the Battle of Alexandria

In 1801, General Sir Ralph Abercromby was given command of a force tasked with ejecting Napoleon from Egypt. He was a perfect choice for the job: he had gained experience of seaborne invasions in the West Indies; he was well-liked in the country and in the army; and he was an extremely efficient commander. On March 8th, 1801, Abercromby's force landed on the beach at Abukir in the face of fierce opposition from French forces entrenched in the dunes. It was a brilliant but costly assault, a kind of premonition of D-Day. One thousand British troops, a fifth of the entire force, were killed getting ashore.

But Abercromby's force gained

a beachhead and marched on to Alexandria, where a pitched battle was fought in the shadow of the old Roman fort. In the course of this battle the 28th Foot (North Gloucestershire) Regiment found itself in a position with the French infantry to the front of them, and the French cavalry to the rear. A lieutenant-colonel Chambers gave the order 'Front rank stay as you are, rear rank about turn!'. The 28th beat the French back on two fronts, and the Gloucester Regiment earned the right – unique in the British army – of wearing a badge on both the front and the back of their caps.

In the midst of the battle, Abercromby himself was mortally wounded by a spent bullet. As he was carried off the battlefield, a soldier's blanket was placed under his head as a pillow. It seemed to make him more comfortable, and he asked what it was. 'Just a soldier's blanket,' he was told.

'Whose blanket is it?' 'It belongs to one of the men,' came the reply. 'I wish to know to whom the blanket belongs,' insisted Abercromby, and someone was sent to find out where exactly it had come from. 'The blanket belongs to Duncan Roy, a soldier of the 42nd.' 'Then see that Duncan Roy gets his blanket back this night,' said the dying general.

The Deadly Men of Gwent
Welsh archers in the fight against the English

In the early Middle Ages, the Welsh were known as the finest bowmen in the British Isles, and the men of Gwent were the best of the Welsh. A chronicler named Gerald of Wales, writing in 1188, left this impressive and rather gory account of prowess in a recent war against England:

'In this capture by stratagem of Abergavenny Castle, two men-at-arms were rushing across a bridge to take refuge in the tower… The Welsh shot at them from behind, and with the arrows that sped from their bows they actually penetrated the oak doorway of the tower, which was almost as thick as a man's palm. As a permanent reminder of the strength of the impact, the arrows have been left sticking in the door just where their iron heads struck. William de Braose [the English lord of Abergavenny] testifies that, in the war against the Welsh… an arrow pinned the thigh of a soldier to his saddle, although the skirt of his leather tunic was there to protect him outside and inside the leg. He tugged on the reins and pulled his horse round in a half circle, whereupon another arrow, shot by the same bowman, hit him in exactly the same place in the other thigh, so that he was skewered to his horse on both sides. It is difficult to see what more you could do, even if you had a crossbow…'

BOMBS AWAY
The Allies dropped 2.7 million tons of bombs on Europe in the course of the Second World War. Two-thirds of that total was dropped after D-Day, June 6th, 1944. In all, about 100,000 men were

lost by the United States Army Air Force and the RAF's Bomber Command combined. The official death toll for Bomber Command alone was 55,573.

The Burning of Washington
British troops sack the US capital

The United States has so long been a military ally of Britain, it is easy to forget that the two nations have fought against each other – and not just in the war of independence. The Anglo-American war of 1812 was the culmination of a long period of rancour between the United States and the British Empire, caused partly by America's unwillingness to curb relations with the French, whom the British had been fighting for a decade.

The war was bitterly fought. At its height an English fleet blockaded the Atlantic coast of the United States and launched a series of raids. The most infamous of these was directed against Washington DC. The incident is known as the 'Burning of Washington', but the action taken

against the city was more measured, less chaotic, than that epithet implies. The British force, under the command of Rear-Admiral George Cockburn and General Robert Ross, marched into Washington unopposed, having defeated an American army *en route* at the battle of Bladensburg. President James Madison, along with his government and many of the residents, fled into the uplands of Virginia before the attacking force got there: the British occupied a mostly empty city.

But not entirely empty. As the British column, carrying a flag of truce, reached the intersection of Maryland Avenue and Constitution Avenue it was fired upon by partisans from the upper floors of a house on the corner. One bullet pierced the flag. It was small incident, but it infuriated the British soldiers, many of whom were hardened veterans of the Peninsula War.

The outrage of the British goes some way to explaining what followed. The column marched on to the newly built Capitol building, which housed the Senate and the Congress, and put it to the torch. The

Library of Congress with all its many books and historical documents, went up in flames.

The British attackers were under strict order from Cockburn not to damage any private property; his aim was to disable the American administration – and to demoralise the American people – by destroying the architectural centres and symbols of government. But Cockburn intended to make an exception for the offices of *National Intelligencer*, an anti-British newspaper that had been heaping personal abuse on him throughout the war.

He went to some lengths to locate the building where the newspaper was printed, and ordered it to be burned down. Before the order could be carried out, he was approached by some American ladies who lived close by; they entreated him not to burn the building, since their homes were bound to catch fire too. Cockburn, true to his own orders, told his men to tear the building down brick by brick. He was then told by an American that the building belonged not to the newspaper, but to a local judge who was known to be pro-

British. So Cockburn told his men merely to ransack the interior; but he gave them special orders to destroy all the letter 'C's in the press, so that the paper would no longer be able to print his name.

From the newspaper offices, the British headed north to their main target, the White House itself. Dolley Madison, the president's wife, was still inside as the British approached. She was frantically gathering documents and other items of historic importance. She left the building at the back almost as British troops came in through the front.

It is often said that her last act before departing was to cut a lifesize portrait of George Washington from its frame, though this legend is disputed by one of the president's

slaves – a man named Paul Jennings – who stated that the portrait was saved and sent on its way some time before the marauding British came through the door.

When the British did arrive, they found to their delight that a sumptuous supper for forty was laid and ready in the dining room. They ate the meal intended for others, then they burned the White House down.

The British troops left the city within a day of arriving, and all that they had destroyed was soon rebuilt. But the day they had Washington at their mercy – August 25th, 1812 – is the only occasion on which the US capital has ever been in the hands of a foreign enemy.

The Scabbard Discarded
American responses to the British invasion

The Anglo-American war of 1812 was still going on two years later. In September 1814, British ships attacked the city of Baltimore. In the course of the assault they bombarded Fort McHenry, which stood at the entrance to the harbour. An American flag, increasingly tattered, continued to fly throughout the shelling, which lasted for more than 24 hours.

Early in the morning on the day after the bombardment ended, that ragged flag was spotted by Francis Scott Key. He was an American lawyer who had been allowed aboard a British ship to negotiate the release of prisoners. He had enjoyed a pleasant dinner the previous night with Ross and Cockburn, the men who had torched the White House. But now the sight of the fluttering flag inspired Key to write a poem, *The Defence of Fort McHenry*. His first draft was made on an envelope while he was still aboard the enemy ship. The first stanza of that poem was later adopted as America's national anthem – *The Star-Spangled Banner*.

Late in 1814, and in a different theatre of the war, a less well-known but equally memorable statement of American patriotism was made. In December, the British were set to attack New Orleans, which was being defended by forces under General Andrew Jackson (later the seventh president of the United States). During a lull in the fighting a British officer, Harry Smith, was sent out with a party of men to bury the dead and collect the wounded. He was met in the field by a Colonel Butler, Jackson's adjutant-general.

Smith noticed that Butler was carrying a naked sword as if ready to fight – which struck him as rather unseemly, since they were both under a flag of truce. As they stood amid the dead and dying, Smith reproached his enemy: 'What do you carry a drawn sword for?' he said. 'Because,' replied Butler, 'I reckon a scabbard is of no use so long as one of you Britishers is on our soil. We don't wish to shoot you, but we must if you molest our property. We have thrown away the scabbard.'

Few New Brits and Many Old Tashes
The fighting men of Waterloo

Waterloo made Britain the supreme military power in Europe. But only 24,000 of the 67,000 troops under Wellington's command at the battle were British. The rest were drawn from the German states of Prussia, Hannover and Brunswick, along with contingents of Belgians and Dutchmen.

What's more, most of the British soldiers were relatively raw recruits, since nearly all the old soldiers that had fought with Wellington in Spain were in the Americas. Napoleon's army, on the other hand, consisted almost entirely of veterans – *vieux moustaches* or 'Old Moustaches', as they were known. They were devoted to the Emperor and knew that this was the last throw of the dice. They had something to fight and die for, and they fully expected to win. Waterloo was one occasion when the intangible battlefield advantages of confidence and experience did not deliver a victory.

The Doomed Belgrano
Life and death of a warship

The *General Belgrano* was an Argentine cruiser sunk by a volley of torpedoes from a British submarine on May 2nd, 1982, during the Falklands War. It was a controversial incident because the ship was outside the British exclusion zone at the time, and seemed to be steaming away from the islands. The captain of the British submarine felt that the Argentinian ship might nevertheless be able to reach a point where it could harass the British naval task force. His concerns were relayed to London, and the decision to attack was taken personally by the prime minister Margaret Thatcher.

When the sinking was reported in the newspapers, *The Sun* headlined the story with the single word

'GOTCHA', printed in huge type on the front page. Below the headline was a graphic photograph of the ship exploding, its shape silhouetted against the fireball rising from the deck. The Argentinian government was outraged both by the attack and the apparently jubilant reaction of the British press. Many British citizens, meanwhile, were troubled and appalled that a newspaper should gloat in such a way over the deaths of 323 sailors – even if they were enemy combatants.

The question of whether it was proper to sink the ship has never been entirely resolved. The recriminations and soul-searching continued for years after the war was over. In the midst of the debate, a strange fact emerged about the *Belgrano* itself. It turned out the ship had been sold to Argentina by the

United States. When it was an American vessel it had gone under the name of the USS *Phoenix*, and was in fact a survivor of the Japanese attack on Pearl Harbor in 1941.

CANNONBALL COURTESY

The cannonballs used in 18th- and 19th-century guns were relatively slow-moving things. A soldier facing a cannonade could see a ball coming, and if he was quick enough, get out of the way. There is a story of General William Medows, who fought against Tipu Sultan ('The Tiger of Mysore') in the Mysore wars. He was riding down a road when he saw a large ball, a 24-pounder, heading towards him from one side. He stopped his horse, and the ball flew by just in front of him. Had he not come to a halt, it would certainly have killed him. As it was, he doffed his hat to the passing cannonball and said 'I beg you to proceed, sir. I never dispute precedence with any gentleman of your family.'

'By God, Sir, I've Lost My Leg...'
Lord Uxbridge's heroic misfortune at Waterloo

Perhaps the best-known anecdote in British military history concerns the aristocratic *sang-froid* of Lord Uxbridge. The story is told of how a cannonball took off his leg as he sat in the saddle, watching the Battle of Waterloo from a distance. 'By God, sir, I've lost my leg,' he said to the Duke of Wellington, who was next to him. 'By God, sir,' replied Wellington, 'So you have.'

That conversation is apocryphal, but it is true that Uxbridge lost his leg at Waterloo – and the firsthand accounts of his cool courage that day are, if anything, more astounding than the legend.

Uxbridge was, despite the story, no bystander at Waterloo. He was in the thick of the fighting for most of the day, and personally led a charge of the Household Brigade at one of the critical points of the battle. It was a small miracle that he had come through the afternoon unscathed, since several horses had been killed under him as he rallied his troops in the field. The volley that wounded him was almost the last of the day from the French lines. Wellington later said that it passed over his horse's head from the right-hand side before striking Uxbridge in the leg – which implies that the two men were some distance apart – though perhaps close enough to speak to each other. Uxbridge later said that the Duke grabbed him after he was hit, and kept him from falling from the saddle.

And it was not a cannonball that hit Uxbridge, but a volley of grapeshot. It did not take his leg

clean off, it shattered his kneecap and mangled his lower leg. This was without doubt a life-threatening injury. Uxbridge was carried back from the front line to the village of Waterloo, to a house belonging to a man named Hyacinthe Paris. Here he was examined by surgeons, who told him that the only option was to amputate. 'Well gentlemen,' he said. 'I thought so myself. I have put myself in your hands. The sooner it is done, the better.'

While the doctors made ready, Uxbridge chatted with his staff – mostly about the successful outcome of the day. He remarked that such a victory was surely worth a leg. He calmly endured the operation – there was no anaesthetic of course – but he said at one point that the knives seemed to him a little blunt.

Late in the evening, Uxbridge was visited by Sir Hussey Vivian, commander of the 6th Brigade of the Cavalry Division. 'Vivian, take a look at that leg and tell me what you think of it,' requested Uxbridge. 'Some time hence, perhaps, I may be inclined to imagine it might have been saved, and I should like your opinion on it.'

Vivian examined the severed limb, with its splintered bone and lacerated flesh, and told Uxbridge that he was definitely better off without it.

Lord Uxbridge was made Marquess of Anglesey a few days after the battle, and he was awarded the Knight Grand Cross, the highest rank of the Order of the Bath. He was also offered annual compensation of £1,200 for the loss of his leg – which he refused. That leg pension would have added up to quite a sum, since Uxbridge lived well into his eighties. Some years after the battle he revisited the house in Waterloo with his sons, and found that the table that he had lain on for the amputation was still there. He and his boys ate their dinner off it.

As for the leg, it went on to achieve a strange kind of celebrity of its own. Monsieur Paris, the owner of the house where it was sawn off, had asked Uxbridge if he could keep it. Uxbridge assented, and the leg was placed in a little coffin, and buried in the garden beside a willow tree. A tombstone was placed on the spot: 'Here lies buried the leg of the illustrious and valiant Lord Uxbridge...' The grave of the leg became a tourist attraction, and made a good deal of money for its new owners for many years after the battle. What became of it in the end is a matter of dispute. Some accounts say it is still buried in Waterloo village beneath a bed of Waterloo roses (the house of M. Paris is now gone). There is also a story that the leg was exposed above ground when the willow tree next to it blew down in a storm, after which it was for some years displayed inside the house. According to this version, Lord Uxbridge's son (his father now long dead) got to hear of it, and demanded that the leg – or rather the bone – be returned to his family. He was outraged when the incumbent M. Paris offered to sell it to him. A third story says that the leg was deliberately disinterred when Lord Uxbridge died in 1854, brought to England, and re-buried with the rest of his heroic, tired old bones.

A WAR IN NUMBERS
In purely statistical terms, the Great War was a massive upheaval for the British army, and a time of unprecedented expansion. At the

outbreak of the First World War in 1914, Britain's army consisted of just over a quarter of a million men – of whom about 80,000 were stationed in India. By the end of the war, Britain had about 3.5 million men in uniform at home and abroad, and so had grown about 14 times larger. To this total one must add the sad statistic of 700,000, which is the number of men who wore a British uniform in the course of the war, but did not live to see the Armistice.

The Quickest Way to End a War...

Some writers and military men on the business of war

When things look bad and one's difficulties appear great, the best tonic is to consider those of the enemy.
   General Archibald Wavell

★

Rule One on page one of the book of war is: 'Do not march on Moscow'.
   General Bernard Law Montgomery

★

War is all hell.
   General William Sherman

★

The fittest man to make a soldier is a perfect gentleman; for generous spirits are ever aptest for great designs.
   Francis Markham

★

In peace there's nothing so becomes a man
As modest stillness and humility;
But when the blast of war blows in our ears,
Then imitate the action of the tiger:
Stiffen the sinews, summon up the blood,
Disguise fair nature with hard-favoured rage;
Then lend the eye a terrible aspect
   William Shakespeare (Henry V)

★

For a soldier I listed to grow great in fame, and be shot at for sixpence a day.
   Charles Dibdin

★

The quickest way of ending a war is to lose it.
   George Orwell

★

No soldier can fight until he is properly fed on beef and beer.
   The Duke of Marlborough (attrib.)

★

The essence of war is violence…
moderation in war is imbecility.

Thomas Macaulay

WOUNDED HORSES

After the Battle of Waterloo, the horses of the Household Cavalry that had sustained wounds in the fray were gathered together and sold at auction. The anatomist Sir Astley Cooper, soon to become the personal doctor of George IV, bought a dozen of the injured animals, and had them taken to his estate in Hertfordshire. Here he cared for the horses as assiduously as he looked after his human patients. He treated their wounds, and removed buckets of bullets and grapeshot from their bodies. When the horses seemed well enough, Cooper released them into the park. He was surprised, one morning soon after, to see the twelve warhorses form up into a line and charge, as if reliving the battle. These equine veterans of Waterloo repeated their little martial ritual every day, for the rest of their lives.

'You Cannot Conquer America'
The impossible-to-win War of Independence

It was the Earl of Chatham (formerly the British prime minister) who declared in the course of the American War of Independence that Britain was fighting a losing battle. He said baldly that 'you cannot conquer America', and in the event, no-one ever has. Chatham, in one of his speeches on rebellion in the

colonies, even went so far as to say that if he were an American, he would never lay down his arms.

But the very impossibility of winning the conflict outright made the American revolutionary war crueller than it might have been. British troops were inclined to take out their exasperation on the Americans who, as 'rebels', were not seen to be entitled to the same courtesies as a foreign enemy. To the army on the ground, the guerilla tactics used against them seemed like dirty tricks. When an individual redcoat was picked off by a sharpshooter, his comrades were inclined to take retribution on the civilian population. Many times, the British command had to issue orders reminding the troops that they were forbidden to harass or abuse non-combatants.

The Americans believed it was common practice among the British to bayonet wounded enemies where they lay in the field after a battle. Conversely, there were rumours after the Battle of Lexington that the rebels had scalped a captured British captain. One officer, whose contempt for the

rebels knew no bounds, suggested that it would be a good idea to shoot at them with arrows dipped in a tincture of smallpox. In other words, he was advocating biological warfare almost two centuries before the term was invented.

The Face of Kitchener
Harvesting volunteers for the trenches

On August 6th, 1914, two days after the outbreak of the First

JOIN YOUR COUNTRY'S ARMY!
GOD SAVE THE KING

Reproduced by permission of LONDON OPINION

World War, parliament authorised the recruitment of half a million men to serve in the army. It took a mere six weeks to sign up that vast number of raw soldiers. By the end of 1915, two and half million had volunteered for the front.

The rapid and enthusiastic filling of the army lists was due in no small part to the efforts of Field Marshall Lord Kitchener. He was secretary of state for war, and he was the stern face of the recruitment drive. Everybody is familiar with the image of him – moustachioed, unsmiling, sometimes with one finger pointing at the viewer. It has been parodied a hundred times in the century since it first appeared on billboards and in shop windows across the land.

It is usually supposed that the exhortation accompanying Kitchener's impassive features was 'Your Country Needs YOU!' – and this too has become something of a cliché. In fact, the original message was less urgent and not so succinct: 'Britons, Kitchener wants you. Join your country's army! God save the King.' The actual word Kitchener was not present: it was implied by

his picture. And of course it was the picture, not the words, that did the trick. That jabbing forefinger looked like personal encouragement to those who were willing to join up, and like an accusation of cowardice to those who were hesitant about it. The face of Kitchener turned out to be a very far-reaching piece of war propaganda, far more effective than anything that Kitchener did in his role as a government minister. Or as prime minister HH Asquith put it at the time: 'He is not a great man, but he is a great poster.'

The Flagstaff Affair
The absurd casus belli of the Maori War

The Maori War of 1845, also known as the Flagstaff War, was a violent dispute between Britain and the Maori people of New Zealand. It was in essence a colonial war: Britain wanted to take possession of the islands and control trade, and the Maoris were not prepared to give these things up.

But the spark that ignited ten months of fighting between Britain

and the Maoris was something strange and unexpected.

When the British established themselves in the Bay of Islands, in New Zealand's North Island, a Maori chief named Hone Heke had presented a flagpole to the British resident at the trading town of Kororareka (now known as Russell). Later, when relations with the British were on the slide, Hone Heke raided the town to kidnap a Maori woman who had once been a servant of his, and had now become the wife of the local butcher. A rumour had reached the chief that she had described him insultingly as a 'pig's head'. As an afterthought, and as a sign of his displeasure, he chopped down the flagpole that he had gifted to the British in happier times.

The British, for their part, saw the destruction of the flagpole as a deliberate challenge to their sovereignty, and as a snook cocked at the person of Queen Victoria. A new pole was erected, and 170 men of the 99th Lanarkshire Regiment detailed to guard it – but Hone Heke found an opportunity to chop the pole down again. A third pole was erected,

and that was chopped down too.

The fourth flagpole was made of the mizzen mast of a ship, and covered at its base with an iron sleeve. A blockhouse was built around it, and defensive trenches were dug around the blockhouse. On March 11th, 1845, Hone Heke ambushed the British guard with a raiding party. A second Maori detachment attacked the town below Flagstaff Hill as a diversion. The ambush employed the time-honoured Maori tactics. A first wave of fighters would rush forward and, as they passed through the enemy ranks, they would strike a single blow at a single enemy, using clubs edged with razor-sharp coral. A second wave coming hard on the heels would deliver the killer blow to the stunned and wounded opponents before they had a chance to recover. The plan worked, the tactics had the desired effect, and the flagpole was felled like a tree for the fourth time.

In the eyes of the British military the matter of the flagstaff had now become a full-scale rebellion. A large force was sent from Australia to reinforce the British garrison and pursue Hone Heke. But the Maoris were well disciplined and organised, and they had recourse to a number of fortified stockades known as *pa*. The war now turned into a series of sieges of these *pa*, each one stronger and more impregnable than the last. Britain's armed forces found themselves in a common colonial dilemma: they could not defeat their enemy in open battle; but they could not disengage without losing face.

But the war did end – after much bloodshed, and in as bizarre a fashion as it had begun. The rebels were ensconced in a *pa* by the name of Ruapekapeka, 'the bat's nest'. The British were camped outside in large numbers, and heavy guns had been brought up to try and blast the Maori fortification apart. A month into the siege, the artillery had caused considerable damage to the palisade, but the defenders remained firm, and the attackers did not yet dare to make a frontal assault. Then, on the morning of Sunday January 11th, 1846, a British scout noticed that the *pa* seemed unusually quiet. He crept over the damaged barricades and found that the fort was deserted.

All the rebel Maoris, converts to Christianity, were at that moment holding an open-air church service in a glade beyond the far wall of the fortress. They had assumed that their British enemy, since they too were Christians, would not think of attacking an enemy on the Sabbath day. This was of course a fatal overestimate of the piety of the British Army. When the Maoris returned from their prayers they found soldiers swarming into their citadel. There was a fierce fight, but overwhelming numbers and the element of surprise gave the victory to the British. The Maoris who survived the battle melted into the forest – Hone Heke among them. He had lost his war – British firepower and weight of numbers was bound to win out in the end – but the sorry flagpole at Kororareka was not re-erected in his lifetime.

The Face of the Enemy
British soldiers and others pay their respects to their opponents

It is a strange fact of war that the soldiers often acquire a grudging respect for the enemy, however

soldiers better than anyone, put these words into the mouth of a fictional infantryman: *'So 'ere's to you fuzzy-wuzzy / At your home in the Soudan, / You're a pore benighted 'eathen, / But a first-class fighting man.'*

Many real combat soldiers have expressed similar sentiments down the years. Here are some British soldiers, statesmen and others giving their views of Britain's battlefield enemies:

'The most fierce, brave, daring and unmerciful race of men in the world.'
A sergeant of the 18th Hussars, on the Dervish fighters of the Mahdist War

★

'We have a very daring and skilful opponent against us, and, may I say across the havoc of war, a great general.'
Churchill on Erwin Rommel

★

much the official propaganda tries to dehumanise them. This was never truer than at the height of Empire, when British forces were often fighting people seen at home as 'inferior races'.

The soldiers who fought to build and protect the British Empire rarely made the mistake of underestimating the men that they were tasked to fight and kill, the tribal peoples of Africa, India and elsewhere. Rudyard Kipling, who understood British

'Not one man could get near enough to use his spear. It was an awful sight, and as an exhibition of pluck, or rather fanaticism, it could not be equalled.'
Civilian witness of the Battle of Tamai in the Sudan, 1884

★

'They were quiet, and seemed to bear pain well, no groaning or crying out. We could not do anything for them except give them water to drink.'

Captain William Molyneux, describing Zulu wounded, 1879

★

"When the British shoot, the Germans duck; when the Germans shoot, the British duck; when the Americans shoot, everybody ducks....."

World War II joke

★

Zeppelins and Other Outrages
The first inklings of total war

The war that was supposed to be over by Christmas 1914 took a terrifying turn just as the season of peace and goodwill came around. In the fourth month of war, German forces launched an attack on the civilian population of a largely undefended and strategically insignificant town. This was a new kind of warfare – one that assumed that all assets and citizens of the enemy nation were legitimate targets. In the next war, both sides would attack each other's cities, but for now the German action seemed like a moral outrage, clear proof of barbarity.

The attack came early on the morning of December 16th. Four German cruisers were spotted off the coast of Hartlepool at about 8 o'clock in the morning, and soon after they began to fire shells indiscriminately into the town. The bombardment continued for half an hour. By that time Royal Navy vessels were on their way to engage the enemy, but the German cruisers

**THESE PREMISES
WERE TOTALLY DESTROYED
BY A
ZEPPELIN RAID
DURING THE WORLD WAR
ON
SEPTEMBER 8ᵗʰ 1915
REBUILT 1917**

JOHN PHILLIPS
GOVERNING DIRECTOR

were too fast. They steamed off to the north, and the Navy never caught up with them. Similar attacks took place at Scarborough and Whitby, killing a total of 137 people and wounding almost 600 more. Among the casualties in Hartlepool were a mother and her six small children, all killed by a direct hit on their house. The woman's husband was killed elsewhere that same morning – by a shell that hit his workplace.

'One victim,' wrote *The Times*, 'was an old woman who had in her pocket a half-crown and a shilling, both of which, strange to say, were cut right in half.' It is telling that such a frivolously macabre detail seemed

newsworthy: nobody had experienced this kind of warfare before.

That was not the last such outrage. In 1915, Zeppelins dropped bombs for the first time, on the coastal towns of King's Lynn and Great Yarmouth. It seemed a perversely warlike use of the new aerial technology, and was all the more chilling for that. Yet still worse was to come: by 1917, fast-moving German aeroplanes were carrying out bombing raids over the British capital. In the summer of that year, more than 150 Londoners were killed by bombs dropped from planes, and around 400 were injured. The British government issued leaflets with silhouettes of both German and British airships and planes, so that citizens would not be alarmed by the sight of their own aircraft overhead, and would know to take cover if the buzzing biplane in the sky was an enemy one. But the Germans had taken to raiding under cover of darkness: there was no easy way of knowing if the plane that you heard was there to protect you, or to try to kill you.

The government leaflets also advised the more naïve elements of the civilian population not to stand around in crowds while an air raid was in progress, and not to touch unexploded shells. By the time the next war came around, no-one needed telling. People had heard and understood Stanley Baldwin's grim prediction that 'the bomber will always get through', and they knew what to do when it did.

The Blitz of the Second World War was a battle fought by men and women on the ground as much as by pilots and navigators in the air. And this time, the damage and loss of life rained down from the air made the casualties of the First World War look like nothing at all, a mere scratch on Britain's little finger.

FRIEND OR FOE

Lord Raglan was 68 years old when he was promoted to general and put in command of the British forces in the Crimea. He had enjoyed a distinguished career at the Duke of Wellington's side in the Peninsular War, and he had lost an arm at Waterloo. But 40 years had passed, and Raglan was now aged and increasingly absent-minded. He

constantly forgot that he was fighting the Russians, and often referred to the enemy as 'the French'. This was galling for Marshall Canrobert, commander of the French forces that were fighting alongside the British against the Russians.

Britain's Wars in the 19th Century
All the wars that Britain engaged in during the century of empire

The French Revolutionary Wars
(1793–1802, Low Countries, Italy, German Rhineland)

The Napoleonic Wars
(1803–1815, throughout Europe)

The First Kandy War
(1803–1805, Ceylon)

The Second Maratha War
(1803–1805, India)

The Vellore Mutiny
(1806, India)

The Dutch Java War
(1810–1811)

The American War of 1812
(1812–1815, United States, Atlantic waters)

The Nepalese War (1814–1816)

The Second Kandy War (1815)

The Third Maratha War
(1817–1818)

The First Burmese War
(1823–1826)

The Canada Rebellions (1837)

The Syrian War
(1839–1840, modern Lebanon)

The First Afghan War
(1839–1842)

The First Opium War
(1839–1842, China)

The Gwalior Campaign
(1843, India)

The First Sikh War
(1845–1846, India)

The Maori Wars
(1845–1872, New Zealand)

The Second Anglo-Sikh War
(1848–1849, India)

The Second Anglo-Burmese War (1852)

The Crimean War
(1854–1856, Russia)

The Second Opium War
(1856–1860)

The Persian War
(1856–1857, modern Iran, Iraq)

The Indian Rebellion
(1857)

The Pig and Potato War
(1859, San Juan Islands in
North America)

The Bhutanese War
(1865)

The Second Afghan War
(1878–1880)

The Zulu War
(1879, South Africa)

The First Boer War
(1880–1881, South Africa)

The Basuto Gun War
(1880–1881, modern Lesotho)

The Mahdist War
(1881–1899, Sudan)

The Third Anglo–Burmese War
(1885–1887)

The Anglo–Zanzibar Conflict
(1896)

The Second Boer War
(1899–1902)

First Fishguard,
then the World
*The final, farcical invasion
of Britain*

In 1797, as revolution took hold in
France, a naval force set out from
the Continent to invade the British
Isles. One part of the flotilla was to
land in Ireland, and link up with
anti-English elements there; a second
section was to land at Newcastle,
and a third at Bristol. The two forces
on the mainland were supposed to
march towards each other, rallying the
peasantry and the workers in support
of a popular uprising as they went.
Together the French soldiers and the
English rebels would bring down the

government and the crown.

It didn't work out quite that way. Two of the three fleets failed to make it to Britain. Only the four French warships headed for Bristol got as far as the coast, but adverse winds and the currents in the Bristol Channel kept them from getting close to the city. The commander of this French force was an Irish-American named William Tate. Some of his officers were Irish, and much of his 1,400-strong force of fighting men consisted of French convicts. Tate gave up on Bristol, and took the decision to head north, around the Welsh coast for Cardigan Bay. *En route*, Tate captured a sloop named *Britannia*, which must have seemed like a good omen. But the captain of the ship, John Owen, had the good sense to feed Tate some disinformation. He told the commander that Fishguard, Tate's intended target, was well defended with artillery, cavalry and infantry. So on reaching Fishguard, Tate sent one of his ships tentatively towards the harbour. Sure enough, a cannon fired from the fort. The shot was a blank, fired most probably as a salute (the ship was mendaciously

flying the Union Jack). But Tate thought better of risking it, and took his small fleet a small way up the coast to an empty bay, where his men disembarked with their weapons.

Meanwhile the alarm had been raised ashore. A messenger was sent out into the night in search of the lieutenant colonel of the Pembrokeshire Militia, a man named Thomas Knox. The 28-year-old Knox, despite his high rank, had no military experience at all. He had bought his commission, and been placed in command of the militia by his father, a rich landowner, who had also paid out of his own pocket to equip his son's regiment.

The day after the French ships were sighted, the younger Knox arrived at Fishguard with about 200 militiamen. Tate had by now moved inland, and was occupying some high ground near the coast. Some of the Frenchmen had gone foraging for food, and to Tate's great misfortune they found a stock of Portuguese wine, recently salvaged from a wreck. Before long, a significant part of Tate's invasion force was entirely drunk, militarily incapable and mostly elsewhere. So little threat did they pose that one local woman, a shoemaker by the name of Jemima Nicholas, single-handedly took 12 Frenchmen prisoner with a pitchfork, and marched them into Fishguard. The revolutionary invasion was already falling apart.

Everything seemed to conspire against Tate and his invaders. For example, many local people had come out to fight the French or at least watch the spectacle, and it seems that the mass of Welsh womenfolk, in their traditional scarlet capes and black hats, looked at a distance like contingents of red-coated infantrymen. This had an utterly demoralising effect on the dwindling French force. After an uncomfortable night in the open, Tate decided that the game was up, and surrendered without a fight.

Thus ended, or rather fizzled out, the last invasion of Britain. Fifty years after the event, the Pembrokeshire Yeomanry (as the Militia were now known) were awarded the battle honour Fishguard – the only such honour ever bestowed for an action in the United Kingdom.

THE HUMAN COST OF WORLD WAR II

According to the best available statistics, Britain and the Commonwealth suffered 575,000 military deaths in the Second World War. Many of those soldiers, sailors and airmen are buried in one of the 559 official war cemeteries that are to be found in every corner of the globe. The number of civilian dead from Britain and the Commonwealth is held to be 1,568,500. The total death toll of the war – military and civilian for all combatant nations – is an impossible number to calculate. Estimates vary from 55 million to around 70 million.

Whipping and Flogging
Crime and punishment in the ranks

There was a technical difference between 'whipping', which was

Throughout the 18th century and well in the 19th, corporal punishment was a fact of life in the British army and in the Royal Navy. There was a technical difference between 'whipping', which was administered with a rod, and 'flogging', which was done with a rope or lash. The usual minimum sentence for minor offences was 25 strokes with the cat-o-nine-tails. Fifty strokes of the lash was enough to flay all the skin off a man's back.

In the army, floggings were dealt out by the drum-major and his drummers, who took turns to do 25 lashes each, and so never grew tired. The punishment would be carried out before the eyes of the entire regiment *pour encourager les autres* ('to encourage the others'), as Voltaire grimly joked. A regimental doctor was always in attendance, and would examine the victim if he appeared to be on the point of collapse. The doctor had the power to halt the punishment – but this hardly ever happened. Very often, it was the victim who insisted that it go on, because if he did not take his full punishment he was liable to have to receive the balance later, once his wounds had healed.

Up until the Napoleonic wars or thereabouts, corporal punishment in the British Army was subject to a gruesome and grotesque form of

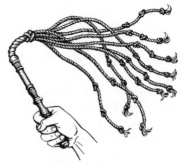

numerical inflation: the number of lashes handed out seems to have grown steadily. A sentence of a hundred lashes became unremarkable; then came instances when men were subjected to 200, 500, 800. Sentences of a thousand lashes were not unheard of, a punishment that amounted to a form of torture, and would have taken perhaps four hours to inflict.

In 1813 sentences above 300 lashes were prohibited – but that ban seems not to have applied everywhere. The most onerous sentence known was handed down some years later to a soldier serving in India: 2,000 lashes. That must surely have proved fatal. All the most dreadful cases took place on the sub-continent. In 1825, a soldier at Dinapore was sentenced to 1,900 lashes, which was reduced by his commanding officer to a more merciful 1,200. In 1814, a soldier of the Bengal European Infantry, on being led out to receive 1,500 lashes, seized the drum major's sword and called upon his fellow soldiers to save him. They declined to do so, and the man received his lashing. He was then court-martialled for mutiny, and shot.

The Four Day's Battle and Other Battles
The naval war against the Dutch

In 1665 war broke out between England and Holland over trading rights in West Africa. It was a ding-dong naval war, in which both sides inflicted a series of heavy blows on the enemy, and then soon after suffered a sound defeat.

England drew first blood when the Royal Navy attacked a Dutch fleet off Lowestoft. It was an easy win: the Dutch flagship was sunk along with 17 other ships, and the remainder of the Dutch fleet could only limp back across the Channel to home ports. Later the same year, an English force attacked a Dutch fleet while it was sheltering in the port of Bergen, then

part of the Danish Empire. The Danes in the forts defending the city were so outraged that the English had brought their quarrel to their waters that they joined in the Dutch bombardment of the English ships, inflicting heavy casualties.

The following summer saw a massive sea-battle in which 84 Dutch ships took on 55 English ones in Flemish waters. The fray lasted from June 11th to June 14th, 1666, a battle that became known as The Four-Day Fight. The noise of the guns was so loud that (as with the artillery of the First World War) their distant boom could be heard in the streets of London. The battle ended in a narrow victory for the Dutch, but a couple of months later Admiral Robert Holmes, commanding a small force of eight ships, happened on the entire Dutch merchant fleet as it lay at anchor in the estuary of the River Vlie. He sent fireships into their midst, with the result that 150 Dutch vessels went up in flames, along with their pungent cargoes of spices. 'Holmes Bonfire', as it became known, was the worst catastrophe ever to befall Dutch shipping.

But Dutch vengeance was terrible. In June 1667, a fleet sailed up the Thames estuary and into the Medway, the coastal inlet where England's busy shipyards were then located. The Dutch ships somehow passed over the great chain that had been laid across the mouth of the Medway specifically to prevent incursions by an enemy, and they wrought havoc at Chatham Docks. There was panic in the streets of London, as rumours spread of a full-scale invasion. In fact, the Dutch action was just a raid, but it was a devastating one. The Dutch captured

The Royal Charles – the ship that a few years before had brought Charles Stuart back from exile to be crowned king – and towed it back to Holland (parts of it can still be seen at the Rijksmuseum in Amsterdam).

The affair was a humiliation for the Royal Navy, perhaps the blackest day in its history. To add insult to injury, many of the crew manning the Dutch ships were English deserters and prisoners-of-war who, as they sailed away, shouted to those ashore that it was good to be serving in a navy that could be bothered to pay their wages.

PERFECT AMITY

In the Napoleonic wars, British officers maintained cordial relations with the enemy – between battles at least. It was a matter of class: a French captain might be an agent of Bonaparte's megalomanic plan for Europe, but he was still a gentleman. The following exchange took place between a British officer and his enemy during the Peninsular War: 'I was posting the night sentries [said the British officer] when I saw a French officer doing the same. I went towards him, and we civilly greeted each other. He came up with the greatest confidence and good humour. I showed him my vedette [guard post], and then remarked that his was too far in advance, and might create an alarm at night when relieving. He said he did not wish to see that, but to please me, if I would point out where I wished he should be, he would immediately move him – which he did. He presented his little flask of excellent French brandy, of which I took a sup, and we parted in perfect amity.

After Rorke's Drift
In the wake of the battle

Eleven Victoria Crosses were awarded to the defenders of Rorke's Drift, the mission station in Natal where, in 1879, 150 men of the 2nd/24th Foot held off as many as 4,000 Zulu warriors. This is the highest number of VCs won in a single action by one regiment. It was a heroic fight by any standards – but the appreciation of the British government was not forthcoming.

When the battle ended, the survivors were in a parlous state. Some were wounded, but nearly all were suffering the effects of firing the Henry-Martini rifle for a prolonged period. The gun had a tendency to grow red-hot in use, so all the combatants had burned fingers, and faces scorched and blackened by smoke. Their chins and shoulders were bruised by the heavy recoil of the rifle. To mitigate the effects of the overheating gun, nearly all the soldiers had resorted to tearing their red tunics into shreds and using them to bind the barrels. No-one had a proper uniform left, so they took the mealie

sacks that had formed part of their makeshift barricade to manufacture rudimentary jerkins: they simply cut holes in the sacks for heads and arms and wore them like smocks.

And so they were attired for some time. It took weeks – and the asking of a question in Parliament – for the men to be issued new uniforms. In Westminster it was eventually decided that each man could have one flannel shirt and a pair of trousers 'cost free' – but not a jacket because they had willfully chosen to destroy what was, after all, government property.

A newspaper satirised this cheeseparing decision with a long poem, the opening lines of which read as follows:

> *There was on old soldier named Dan'el*
> *He fought till his clothes were in rags,*
> *So the government gave him a flannel,*
> *And also a new pair of bags.*
> *And the news it went over the Channel,*
> *Through Europe it's chaff for the wags*
> *That we honour our heroes in flannel,*
> *And clothe their achievements in bags.*

Rabid Wolfe
The madness of a fine general

General Wolfe, the conqueror of Quebec, was often accused in his lifetime of dangerously eccentric behaviour. There is a story that in 1759, shortly before departing England to fight the French in Canada, he dined with prime minister William Pitt and his brother-in-law Lord Temple. After a sip or two of wine Wolfe 'broke forth in a strain of gasconade and bravado. He drew his sword and, as the prime minister watched aghast, rapped the table with it, he flourished it round the room, and he talked of the mighty things which that sword was to achieve.' After Wolfe had gone home, Pitt is said to have lifted his eyes to the heavens and said 'Good God! That, I should have entrusted the fate of the country and of the administration to such hands!'

The story is almost certainly a malicious lie. It is unthinkable that a cultured officer would draw his sword at the dining table, however excited he was about fighting for his country. Equally unfounded is the theory, which was propounded long after Wolfe's death, that he was a suppressed (and somewhat hysterical) homosexual. In any case, what if he was? It clearly didn't prevent him from being a great commander. King George II had it right when he said to the Duke of Newcastle: 'Mad, is he? Then I wish he would bite some of my other generals.'

It is said that on the night before Wolfe led his soldiers up the Heights of Abraham to engage the French,

he recited part of Gray's *Elegy* to his officers. 'Gentlemen,' he said afterwards, 'I would rather have written that poem than take Quebec tomorrow.' But take Quebec he did – and he took three bullets too, in the very moment that the French were set to flight. He was told of his victory as he lay bleeding on the ground. 'I die contented,' he said – and these were his last words.

Bobbie the Mongrel, the Courageous Mascot
How a regimental pet fought like a trooper

When the men of the 66th Regiment of Foot were deployed to Afghanistan in the course of the Second Afghan War, a dog called Bobbie went with them. He was a mongrel belonging to a lance-sergeant named Peter Kelly, and he was adopted as the regimental mascot.

By the summer of 1880, Bobbie and the regiment were installed in barracks in Kandahar. In July, the 66th received orders to form up and march out into the wilderness of the north-west frontier and assist in quelling a

They marched to meet the enemy, and joined battle the next day. The soldiers of the British/Indian column were physically exhausted before the fighting even began, and they were outnumbered by a factor of twelve to one. The battle was a rout: more than two-thirds of the men of the 66th were killed either on the battlefield, or fighting a desperate rearguard action as they withdrew. Bobbie was seen snarling and barking at the enemy in the heat of the battle, but was lost as the column made its brave but disorderly retreat. He was thought dead, but turned up wounded the next day as the survivors of the engagement made their way back to Kandahar – and was reunited with his owner, Lance-Sergeant Kelly, who was also among the wounded.

rebellion led by Ayub Khan, younger brother of the Amir of Afghanistan. The 66th was accompanied by various detachments of the Indian Army – among them the 3rd Sind Horse and the 30th Bombay Native Infantry (known as Jacob's Rifles). The British/Indian column searched for Ayub Khan's rebels for ten days, by which time they were tired and perilously short of water. Bobbie had kept up with his regiment throughout the excursion.

On July 26th, the British brigade received intelligence that Ayub Khan was close to the village of Maiwand.

Somehow, word of the dog that fought at the Battle of Maiwand reached home. When the regiment returned to England, some of the survivors of the battle were granted an audience with Queen Victoria, and they took Bobbie along with them. She apparently listened intently as one of the soldiers told her Bobbie's story, and insisted on seeing the scar on his back where he had been wounded in battle. She presented the mongrel with the Afghan campaign medal, which she pinned to his collar.

But the dog who had survived a murderous encounter with Afghan tribesman was no match for an English city's busy roads. Not long after his homecoming, Bobbie was run over by a hansom cab in Gosport, and killed. His body was stuffed, and put on display at the headquarters of the Berkshire Regiment – the

successor regiment to the 66th Foot. He can still be seen there, the Afghan Medal around his neck.

The Kindness of Nazis
Douglas Bader and the Luftwaffe

Douglas Bader, Spitfire pilot, lost both his legs some years before the Second World War. He had crashed into the ground while practising for an airshow. After a long convalescence marked by almost

superhuman determination, he learned to walk on prosthetic legs, to drive, even to dance.

When war came, Bader offered his services to the RAF and – after persistent cajoling of the authorities – was permitted to fly in combat. He fought gallantly during the retreat from Dunkirk and in the Battle of Britain, but was shot down over France in 1941. When he bailed out of his Spitfire, one of his prosthetic legs became caught in the cockpit, so it was a one-legged Bader that parachuted into enemy territory. He was soon picked up by the Germans, who treated him with great courtesy and respect. Foolishly perhaps, they even allowed him to sit in the cockpit of a Messerschmitt fighter, and try out the controls.

Around this time, before he was despatched to a POW camp, Bader was introduced to the German ace Adolf Galland, with whom he struck up an immediate friendship. It was Galland who arranged for a message to be passed to the RAF, letting them know that Bader was alive, but in need of a new tin leg. An arrangement was made whereby an RAF bomber under escort would be permitted to fly unmolested over German-occupied France, and drop a leg by parachute to a Luftwaffe base close to the POW camp where Bader was being held. This was done a couple of weeks after Bader's capture – though the Luftwaffe were somewhat dismayed when the bomber flew on to carry out a raid on a German target.

Bader spent the rest of the war in captivity. He made several attempts to escape, and got away from his POW camp more than once. At one point the Germans became so exasperated with Bader's escapes that they threatened to take his legs away again to stop him trying. Instead, they sent him to Colditz Castle, where he remained until the end of the war.

By this time, Adolf Galland had become a prisoner-of-war in Britain, having surrendered to the Americans in the last days of the war. Bader went to see him when he returned from Colditz, and in the POW camp he met a German comrade of Galland's who, like Bader himself, was an amputee. Seizing the chance to return Galland's favour, he arranged for this

Luftwaffe pilot to be fitted with a prosthetic leg like his own.

Bloody Richard and Talbot the Terrible
The antiheroes of England's wars

Richard I, known affectionately to English history as the Lionheart, was a figure of terror to the people in whose lands he waged war. For centuries after his crusade in the Middle East, naughty Arab boys were told: 'Don't do that, England will get you.' The name of John Talbot was used in similar fashion in France after the Hundred Years War. Many generations of French children were frightened into obedience with the phrase: *Sois sage, le Talbot viendra* ('Be good, or the Talbot will come').

In life, Talbot was the most feared of English commanders; it was said that aged 88 he rode into battle, wearing no armour, as if the enemy would not dare attack him. In fact he was 66 at most when he died, his head smashed by a Frenchman's axe at the siege of Castillon. Talbot crops up twice in the works of Shakespeare, who places him (erroneously) at

Agincourt. 'Old men forget…' says King Henry before the battle,

…yet all shall be forgot,
But he'll remember with advantages
What feats he did that day: then shall our names.
Familiar in his mouth as household words
Harry the king, Bedford and Exeter,
Warwick and Talbot, Salisbury and Gloucester,
Be in their flowing cups freshly remember'd.

In the little-read play *Henry VI (Part I)* Talbot is a central character, a kind of medieval English Rambo who takes on the French single-handed. 'A stouter champion never handled sword,' the king says of him. The action of the play has Talbot set to win his war until he is brought low by the demonic sorcery of Joan of Arc – who is the villain of the piece.

'In Flanders' Field…'
*The poem that spawned
a sacred tradition*

The wearing of poppies in remembrance of Britain's war dead began in 1921, and immediately became a national tradition. The idea came from a poem, *In Flanders' Field*, written by a Canadian medic named John McCrae. The first two stanzas are as follows:

*In Flanders' fields, the poppies blow
Between the crosses, row on row,
That mark our place; and in the sky
The larks, still bravely singing, fly
Scarce heard amid the guns below…*

We are the Dead. Short days ago

*We lived, felt dawn, saw sunset glow,
Loved, and were loved, and now we lie
In Flanders fields…*

John McCrae wrote the poem in May 1915. There is a legend that he rejected his poem as inferior, and tore the page out of his notebook, only for a fellow officer to rescue it and submit it for publication. One way or another, it found its way to the offices of *Punch* magazine and was published.

The poem quickly captured the public's imagination, and it became immensely popular in the course of the war. Strangely, perhaps, it was widely used in recruiting drives.

McCrae was not the first to notice that red poppies have a tendency to spring up on the broken, war-ploughed earth of Belgian battlefields. Thomas Macaulay had drawn attention to this odd botanical fact while describing the aftermath of the Battle of Landen of 1693, a long-forgotten encounter of the Nine Years War, in which an English army under William III was soundly beaten by the French. 'The next summer the soil, fertilised by twenty thousand corpses, broke forth into millions of poppies,' wrote the Victorian historian.

He then went on to make explicit the metaphorical link between the colour of the flowers and the blood of the dead – something that is left unspoken in McCrae's work: 'The traveller who, on the road from Saint Tron to Tirlemont, saw that vast sheet of rich scarlet spreading from Landen to Neerwinden, could hardly help fancying that the figurative prediction of the Hebrew prophet was literally accomplished, that the earth was disclosing her blood, and refusing to cover the slain.' As for McCrae, he lived to see the success of his poem,

but never witnessed the annual act of remembrance that grew out of it. In January 1918, while still serving with the Canadian Army Medical Corps, he died of pneumonia contracted at the front. He was buried with honours in the military cemetery at Wimereux near Boulogne, where his grave can still be seen.

Dirty Tricks at Stamford Bridge
The other invasion of 1066

The Norman invasion of October 1066 was preceded, less than a month before, by an unsuccessful Viking invasion. In September that year, Norwegians under King Harald Hardrada landed in Yorkshire and foregathered on the River Derwent, at a place known as Stamford Bridge.

The English King Harold Godwinson and his army marched north from London to join battle. They covered 185 miles in just four days, a march so swift that the English took the Vikings completely by surprise. According to some chroniclers, the Vikings had not even got around to unloading their chainmail armour from their ships.

But the invaders fought hard. According to one account, a giant Viking warrior single-handedly halted the English advance by standing on the narrow bridge and swinging his long-handled dane-axe at any Englishman who dared to take him on. The accounts say that he killed 40 English, and held up King Harold's army for a matter of hours. At last, someone came under the bridge in a boat, and thrust a spear up and into

the Norwegian through the gaps in the planking. Even if your heart is with Harold and the English, you can't help feeling sorry for that poor Viking warrior.

Once the champion of Harald Hardrada's army was dispatched, the English quickly overcame the Vikings, and killed the vast majority of them. Three hundred ships had carried the Norwegian host to English shores; twenty-four ships sufficed to take the survivors home. And it was said that the fields around Stamford Bridge were strewn with bleached white bones for a lifetime after the battle.

Britain's Briefest War
The Anglo-Zanzibar conflict

The shortest war in Britain's long history – indeed in any country's history – is the Anglo–Zanzibar War of 1896. It began at 9 o'clock on the morning of August 27th, and was all over by quarter to ten.

The war was precipitated by the death, on August 25th, of the pro-British sultan of Zanzibar. According to the terms of a treaty of 1886, any sultan acceding to the throne had

failed to break the deadlock.

At 9.02, five Royal Navy warships began bombarding the palace. This action constitutes the entire history of the war – but it was not all one-sided. In the harbour with the Royal Navy ships was one vessel belonging to the sultan. It was named HHS *Glasgow*, and it was armed with seven small artillery pieces and a Gatling gun that had been a gift from Queen Victoria to the deceased sultan. The crew of the *Glasgow* began firing on the British ships, which promptly returned fire. The *Glasgow* went down, and its crew were rescued by the Royal Navy.

first to seek British approval. The new man on the throne – Khalid bin Barghash – was disinclined to kowtow to the British in this way. He was the nephew of the deceased sultan, and thought that his right to the throne was clear enough (though many suspected that he had assassinated is uncle). Khalid was issued with an ultimatum: either stand down and leave the palace by 9 o'clock on the 27th, or find himself at war with the British Empire. Khalid chose to stay put inside the palace, and attempted to negotiate a peace via American officials in Zanzibar, but these talks

Meanwhile the palace had caught fire. At some point before 9.30am, the sultan fled to the German Embassy, leaving his slaves and servants to fight on. After the war, diplomatic efforts were made to persuade the German ambassador to surrender Khalid, but he refused. Some months later Khalid escaped from Zanzibar, and went into exile in Dar-Es-Salaam, then part of German East Africa. The British eventually caught up with him in 1916. He was captured when British forces took possession of the city during the African campaign in the First World War.

As for the Anglo-Zanzibar war, it ended between 9.40 and 9.45am, when the shelling of the palace ceased. As many as 500 loyal soldiers of the sultan died inside the burning palace. On the British side, one naval officer was badly wounded, though he made a full recovery. A British force went ashore, occupied the town, and installed their own first choice of sultan – who found that his powers were much reduced, and that he had only a smouldering wreck of a palace to rule from. One of the new sultan's first tasks as ruler was to find the money to reimburse the Royal Navy for the cost of the shells and the bullets that it had expended in the course of bringing him to power.

WCs and Devil's Chariots
How the tank got its name, and first saw action

The origin of the word 'tank' is oddly obscure. Most authorities agree that the name was abbreviated from 'water tank', a term used to keep the invention secret while it was under development in the early months of the First World War.

One version says that workers in factories where prototypes were being assembled were told that they were making water tanks, so as to disguise the secret nature of the task. Another version says that Winston Churchill, then First Lord of the Admiralty, was presented with three possible names for the new weapon: the rather

clumsy but descriptive 'motor-war car', the deliberately obfuscatory 'cistern', or the monosyllabic 'tank'. According to this version of the story, he went for 'tank' because it was the simplest word.

But Churchill himself, in his own writing, put forward another version of the origin of the word tank. According to his account, the blueprints of the earliest tanks were marked with the word 'water carriers'. When it was pointed out that this would naturally abbreviate to 'WCs', the headings were changed to 'water tanks'. While the finished machines were being trialled, they were sometimes referred to in official correspondence as 'landships' – a rather unconvincing metaphor that might owe its existence to the fact that the Admiralty was behind the scheme. When the newfangled tanks were at last deployed in battle, in September 1916, an overawed German newspaper correspondent described them in his despatch as 'the devil's chariots'.

It is true that they were a terrifying newcomer to the churned-up, bomb-blasted battlefields of France. But they were also a perilous and cumbersome way to fight. The first tanks had a crew of eight, four of whom manned the two six-pounder guns, while the rest drove the tank.

Here is one British soldier's description of trying to manoeuvre a Mark I tank at the Battle of Cambrai. While the four gunners 'blazed away, the rest of the perspiring crew kept the tank zigzagging to upset the enemy's aim. [The crew] took their orders by signals. First of all the tank had to stop. A knock on the right side would attract the attention of the right gearsman. The driver would hold out a clenched fist, which was the signal to put the tank into neutral. The gearsmen would repeat the signal to show it was done. The officer, who controlled two brake levers, would pull on the right one, which held the right track. The driver would accelerate, and the tank would slew round slowly on the stationary right track while the left track went into motion. As soon as the tank had turned sufficiently, the procedure was reversed. In between pulls on his brakes, the rank commander fired the machine gun...'

Despite its obvious design faults, the tank clearly had promise as a battlefield weapon. But as soon as the war ended, it was all but forgotten. One British general, speaking in 1919, said of the recent war that 'the tank was a freak. The circumstances that called it into existence were exceptional, and are not likely to recur. If they do, they can be dealt with by other means.' British military thinkers were still wedded to the idea that old-fashioned cavalry, spurs and all, were the best way to exploit a breakthrough by the infantry. Field Marshall Sir Douglas Haig fiercely resisted any effort to downsize the cavalry in the post-war defence cuts (it was said of him that he was bright only to the top of his boots), with the result that tank production ceased altogether. A few visionaries such as Liddell Hart saw that the tank would be a key weapon in any future war, and wrote persuasive and prescient books about its coming role. No-one in the British establishment took any notice of them; but Liddell Hart's views insights made a deep impression on General Heinz Guderian, the German architect of *Blitzkrieg*.

False Craters
How Argentinian troops fooled the RAF

The airport at Port Stanley was a vital resource for the occupying Argentinians during the Falklands War of 1982. Though the runway was too short for fighter jets to use, the airport was the main entry point for military supplies flown in from the Argentinian mainland. So from the British point of view, it was essential that Port Stanley be put out of action.

The RAF mounted many raids on the airport, and made use of satellite photographs to assess their effect. The photographs showed that the runway was pitted with bomb craters – which allowed the British authorities to say that the runways had been entirely churned up and the airport was, in therefore, useless to the enemy.

But the British had been deceived by a very cheap and simple trick. Each night, after a raid, Argentinian soldiers would go out onto the runway with spades and buckets of earth. Working in the dark, they would arrange the dirt in circles of various sizes. It was these circles that were routinely photographed by spy satellites in the course of the following day. To the British military analysts who inspected the satellite images, the improvised circular sandcastles looked convincingly like deep bomb craters. They were nothing of the sort, of course. And it was an easy matter for the Argentinian garrison at the airport to clear away their handiwork each night, and remake it before dawn, so that their supply planes could land in secrecy and safety.

Duck and Dash
The unorthodox tactics of the 42nd Highlanders

Throughout the 18th century, it was standard practice for opposing armies to take their time about arranging themselves on the battlefield. With much pomp and playing of drums, the massed ranks of infantry would line up opposite each other, perhaps 200–300 feet (60–100 metres) apart. When the time came, the riflemen would go through the

laborious process of loading their muskets and then, when the order came, discharge volley after volley into the ranks of the enemy.

It was sometimes the case that entire regiments were virtually annihilated by this stationary but deadly manner of warfare. Only when one army looked to be losing its nerve or its cohesion would an order be given to the other army to charge, at which the battle would descend into close-quarters fighting.

But the 42nd Highland Regiment (later the Black Watch) deployed a distinctively Scottish tactic that was a brilliant response to the usual stand-your-ground-and-die. Their ruse was to load their muskets, wait till the enemy was about to shoot, then fall flat on the ground just as the order to fire was given. If they timed it right, the enemy's bullets flew over their heads. They would smartly jump up and quickly shoot off a volley into the enemy lines. Then, while they were still shrouded in smoke from their own

muskets, and before the enemy could finish reloading, they would rush the enemy lines with their 'claymore and targe' (sword and shield). It was a devastating technique, and worked well on more than one occasion. But old-school English generals saw the Scottish method as unseemly, untraditional, almost unsporting – and they put a stop to it.

Some Martial Firsts...
Pioneering moments in the history of battle

The first serviceman to receive the Victoria Cross was Charles Davis Lucas. In the course of the Crimean war he was serving as mate on HMS *Hecla* off the Aland Islands (far from the Crimean peninsula, off the coast of Finland). A live shell fired from the fort at Bomarsund landed on the deck of his ship.

All hands were ordered to throw themselves flat on the deck, but Lucas ran up and picked up the hissing shell, and threw it overboard. It exploded before it hit the water. Lucas was immediately promoted to lieutenant, and later received his medal, 'For Valour', from the hand of Queen Victoria herself.

★

The first casualty of the Zulu War (1879) was a navy rating who was devoured by a crocodile.

★

The so-called Moonlight Battle, which took place on January 16th 1780, was the first British fleet action to be fought at night.

★

The first doodlebug – Hitler's V-1 flying bomb – was launched on June 13th, 1944, a week after D-Day. It landed on a house in Grove Road, Poplar, east London, killing a couple who lived on the top floor.

★

The first V-2 to fall on Britain landed in Chiswick, west London, on the evening of August 29th, 1944. It killed a 63-year-old woman, a three-year-old child, and a serviceman on leave. The most terrifying thing about V-2s was that they travelled faster than sound – so the explosion came entirely out of the blue, ahead of the whoosh of the missile's approach.

★

Tanks were deployed in battle for the first time on the Somme in August 1916. Some of the first tanks were equipped with cannon, and were known as 'male tanks'; others were armed with machine guns, and were known as female tanks.

★

The first dive by a Royal Navy submarine took place on February 5th, 1902.

★

The first, and also the last, German prisoner ever to escape from a British POW camp was Oberleutnant Gunther Pluschow, who in 1915 absconded from a camp at Donington Hall in Derbyshire, made his way to London, stowed away on a Dutch steamer at Tilbury, talked his way past the Dutch police on his arrival in Holland, then caught a train to Germany. He was given a hero's welcome and the Iron Cross First Class on his arrival. No German POW ever managed to escape to Nazi Germany in the course of the Second World War – but 26,000 of them decided to stay on in Britain after the war's end and make a life for themselves with their former enemy.

★

… And Some Lasts
Final bows in war and battle

The last English king to die in battle was Richard III, at Bosworth Field in 1453. An old tradition says that he died trying to hack his way through the entourage of Henry Tudor to kill his rival and so win the battle with a single blow. Richard was unhorsed as he waded into the fray, and killed by Henry's men as he lay on the ground. Shakespeare gave Richard a magnificent set of last words 'A horse, a horse, my kingdom for a horse.' His actual last moments were rather different according to one contemporary account: 'Although small of body and weak in strength, he most valiantly defended himself as a noble knight to his last breath, often exclaiming as he was betrayed and saying "Treason! Treason! Treason…!"'

★

The last occasion on which regimental colours were carried into action was the Battle of Majuba Hill, which took place on February 27th, 1881, and was the main battle of the First Boer War. After that, the colours were left in England when a regiment went overseas – not in the barracks, but in a church or cathedral of the regiment's own locality.

★

The last-ever charge by the British cavalry is usually held to be the assault made by the 21st Lancers at the Battle of Omdurman in September 1898. Winston Churchill, then 23 years old, took part in the charge, and left a vivid account of what it was like to ride a horse into the thick of the enemy lines: 'The Dervishes fought manfully. They tried to hamstring the horses. They fired their rifles, pressing the muzzles into the very bodies of their opponents. They cut reins and stirrup-leathers. They flung their throwing-spears with great dexterity. They tried every device of cool, determined men practiced in war and familiar with cavalry; and, besides, they swung sharp, heavy swords which bit deep. The hand-to-hand fighting on the further side of the *khor* lasted for perhaps one minute. Then the horses got into their stride again, the pace increased, and the Lancers drew out from among their antagonists. Within two minutes of the collision every living man was clear of the Dervish mass. All who had fallen were cut at with swords till they stopped quivering, but no artistic mutilations were attempted. The enemy's behaviour gave small ground for complaint.'

★

The Last Post – that simple, deeply moving tune – is played every evening at precisely 8 o'clock under the Menin Gate near Ieper (Ypres). Buglers perform the ceremony in commemoration of those who have fallen in war, and have done so every night since 1928. The only break was during the four years that Ypres was under German occupation in the Second World War, for that period, the ceremony was transferred to Brookwood Cemetery near Woking.

★

The last full-scale pitched battle to be fought on British soil was Culloden, in the Scottish highlands, in 1746. It was a crushing defeat for the Jacobite highlanders, about 2,000 of whom were killed or wounded in what was a brief battle. The casualties of the English and their allies amounted to about 300 men.

★

The last British survivor of the Great War was Harry Patch. He was born in 1898, in the village of Combe Down, near Bath, Somerset, and at the age 19 served as a machine-gunner in the trenches. At that time he probably would not have bet much on surviving to his 20th birthday, but in the event he lived to see the entire 20th century. He had a life that spanned three centuries and two millennia, and at the time of his death in 2009 he was – at 111 years of age – the oldest man in Europe. The band Radiohead wrote a song in his memory.

★

60 YEARS ON DUTY

The 18th century was perhaps the worst epoch ever in which to be a career soldier in the British Army. The organisation of the army was appalling – and at times entire regiments could be practically forgotten for decades. The 38th Regiment of Foot, for example, was posted to the West Indies in 1707, and not recalled until almost 60 years later. So to serve with the 38th was, in effect, to be sentenced to a lifetime's exile. When the 38th eventually came home, in 1764, their uniforms were in rags, and had been repaired many times over with bits of old sacking. Later the 38th was incorporated into the South Staffordshire Regiment, and in 1935, their unduly long ordeal in the West Indies was commemorated by the grant of permission to wear the regimental badge on a buff-coloured backing – a little nod to the sacks they were reduced to wearing during their long Caribbean vigil.

Carrots: the RAF's Secret Weapon
The role of root vegetables in the battle for the skies

In the Second World War, the Air Ministry let it be known that the crews of night fighters were getting extra portions of carrots – because carrots, as everyone knew, help you see better in the dark. The policy, it seemed, was working: Luftwaffe commanders were finding that the British were increasingly adept at locating German planes in the night sky and shooting them down.

It was a lie – but one containing elements of truth. For one thing, everyone was growing their own veg, as Britain was more or less blockaded, so everyone was eating more carrots than they might otherwise have done. Secondly, the old wives' tale about carrots and night vision was partly correct: carrots stimulate the body to produce vitamin A, which in turn helps produce a pigment called visual purple that is essential for discerning objects in a poor light.

But the success of the British night fighters had nothing to do with their own eyesight. It was down to Britain's new and highly secret defensive weapon – radar. All along the coast there were radar stations that could detect German bombers 100 miles away. The RAF knew the Luftwaffe was coming, as well as what direction they were coming from and in what kind of numbers. There was plenty of time to get fighters airborne, and send

them into the attack. The ruse did not last for long: the radar stations soon became targets for German bombs. But the carrot story probably bought the beleaguered RAF some time, and saved some flyers' lives.

Top Brass
Rank and seniority in the British armed forces

The army is a rigid hierarchy, and so are the Royal Navy and the RAF. Though the two older services evolved separately, there is a fairly strict correspondence between the army ranks and naval ranks, particularly at officer level. Lieutenant General David Henderson originally proposed that Royal Air Force officers use a combination of British Army and Royal Navy ranks, however, the

War Office argued that the RAF should have its own ranks and the Admiralty opposed any use of their rank titles (*Customs and Traditions of the Royal Air Force*). Here is a comparative table of the ranks in the three services.

ARMY	ROYAL NAVY	ROYAL AIR FORCE
General	Admiral of the Fleet	Marshall of the RAF
Lieutenant General	Vice-Admiral	Air Marshall
Major General	Rear Admiral	Air Vice Marshall
Brigadier	Commodore	Air Commodore
Colonel	Captain	Group Captain
Lieutenant Colonel	Commander	Wing Commander
Major	Lieutenant Commander	Squadron Leader
Captain	Lieutenant	Flight Lieutenant
Lieutenant	–	–
–	Sub-Lieutenant	–
Second Lieutenant	–	Pilot Officer
–	–	Acting Pilot Officer
–	Midshipman	–
Warrant Officer First Class	Warrant Officer	Warrant Officer
Warrant Officer Second Class		
Staff Sergeant	Chief Petty Officer	Flight Sergeant
Sergeant	Petty Officer	Sergeant
Corporal	Leading Seaman	Corporal
Lance Corporal	–	–
–	Able Seaman	Leading Aircraftman
Private	Ordinary Seaman	Aircraftman

Down the centuries, certain military ranks have become extinct. The most junior rank of commissioned officer was once an ensign or (in the cavalry) a cornet. Both terms are taken from the flag or colour that it was their job to carry. The words were dropped in favour of 'second lieutenant' in 1871 as part of the Cardwell reforms of the army. The rank of subaltern was abolished at the same time; it covered both grades of lieutenant, and was deemed to be superfluous.

All of the ranks for army officers have intriguing histories. Lieutenant is French, and means 'holding place' – that is, deputising for a superior officer. Captain is a French word that comes to English via late-Latin, and means simply 'head', in other words, 'leader'. Major is an abbreviation of sergeant-major – originally a higher rank than it is now. The 'major' part, though identical to the classical Latin, is an old-French adjective meaning greater (than a captain). Colonel,

oddly, derives from the Italian *colonello*, 'little column', since the function of a colonel was to lead the regiment as it marched as a column into the field. 'General' is French once again; it is an abbreviation of Captain-General, and so implies that the holder of the rank is head of the entire army.

Sergeant-majors in the modern sense are conspicuously absent from the army list because this is not so much a rank as a job title, a function performed by a warrant officer. Sergeant-majors come in various guises: regimental sergeant-major, company sergeant-major, squadron sergeant-major (in the cavalry), battery sergeant-major (in the Royal Artillery) artificer sergeant-major (in the Royal Electrical and Mechanical Engineers) and mechanist sergeant-major (in the Royal Engineers).

As for the naval and air-force ranks, only 'midshipman' and 'aircraftman' are solidly English in origin. The term 'admiral' derives from the Arabic phrase *amir-al-bahr*, meaning 'commander of the sea', and the various grades of RAF marshall are all in origin 'horsegrooms' (from the Old High German, *marahscalc*).

At the bottom of the hierarchy comes the humble private. Until around 1700, an ordinary soldier was known as a 'private centinel', meaning one of a company of a hundred, but individually responsible only for himself. This was contracted simply to private, while the word sentinel was corrupted to 'sentry' – the role that is the dull drudgery of low-ranking soldiers everywhere, in times of peace and in times of war.

His Majesty the General
George II at the Battle of Dettingen

King George II was at the head of his troops at the Battle of Dettingen of 1743. This was the last occasion on which a British monarch personally took command of his army in battle.

There is a story that some enemy French cavalry came close to capturing the king as he sheltered under an oak tree, but a group of soldiers from the 22nd (Cheshire) Regiment of Foot drove the French horsemen off. The king picked an oak leaf off the tree and handed it to one of the men who had rescued him – a symbolic token of gratitude. The cap badge of the Cheshires featured an acorn and oak leaf throughout the regiment's long history. They wore it with Wolfe at Quebec, when they fought on the Somme, and when they landed on Gold Beach on D-Day. Their story ended in 2004, when they became part of the amalgamated Mercian Regiment.

GREEN AND HAIRY
In 1797 a battalion of the 60th Infantry Regiment was reconstituted as the British army's first rifle corps. They wore a dark green uniform, in imitation of the Austrian Jaegers on whom they were modelled. Entirely incidentally, their coats served as a form of camouflage (but it was many decades before the army as a whole abandoned red in favour of a colour that made men a less conspicuous target for snipers). The men of that first rifle corps had the distinction of being the only soldiers in the army allowed to sport moustaches – and this too was a rather slavish homage to the Austrian custom of the time.

The March of the Sheep
Keeping livestock from the enemy

In the first winter of World War I, there was some concern at the War Office that the Germans might be preparing to mount an invasion of Britain. It fell to the so-called Home Command to take appropriate military precautions for this eventuality.

JFC Fuller, a staff officer attached to the Home Command, was summoned into the presence of his commanding officer, a general, and told that the War Office had decided that all the sheep in the south-eastern counties – several million of them – were to be evacuated to Salisbury Plain if the invasion came, so that they did not fall into enemy hands. It was Fuller's job to make the arrangements. 'I knew this was an impossible task,' wrote Fuller, 'But there was no arguing over it, so I spent days and days working out march tables for sheep. If ever there was a wicked waste of time, this was it.'

Once he had done the paperwork,

Fuller went back to the general and pointed out that all these sheep on the move would block half the roads in the south of England for days on end. 'Of course,' said the general. 'At once arrange to have a number of signposts ready and marked "Sheep not to use this road".'

'But what if the less well-educated sheep are unable to read them,' replied the exasperated Fuller.

LAM to the Slaughter
Bad inventions for the RAF

In the course of the Second World War, huge amounts of ingenuity were expended on devising new weapons. But not all the ideas that got off the drawing board were well thought through. Two of the more questionable ideas for aerial combat

– now almost entirely forgotten – are the device known as a Turbinlite, and a flying bomb called LAM.

Turbinlite was nothing more or less than a huge searchlight attached to the nose of an aircraft, like a headlight. The idea that it would be used in conjunction with radar (then just beginning to be introduced to combat planes) to locate and then illuminate enemy fighters at night. While the German planes were caught in the glare of the turbinlite, Hurricanes would close in and shoot them down. It seems not to have occurred to anyone that the target plane might not obligingly fly straight and steady within the Turbinlite's beam; or that an attacking plane that could direct a searchlight directly at an enemy might as well be shooting a gun at it instead.

LAM was an even worse and rather more bizarre idea. The acronym stood for Long Aerial Mine, and it was essentially a bomb on a rope. The idea was that an explosive charge would be towed behind a Havoc nightfighter on a cable 2,000 feet (600 metres) long. An enemy aircraft flying into the rope would cause the bomb to be drawn against its hull, where it would explode on impact. Again, the obvious failing was ignored: that the tangle of the two aircraft in flight might very well result in both of them crashing to the ground. A final absurdity: the entirely transparent codename for LAM was 'Mutton'.

DISHONEST GAMES FOR ARCHERS

In the reign of Edward I, every English yokel was required by law to do some archery 'at the butts' after church on Sunday. It was this skill, learned in youth, that made the archer such a devastating asset to England in the protracted conflicts of the Hundred Years War. It was said then that an English bowman could pierce an oyster shell at 250 yards. And a good archer could launch 12 arrows a minute, a rate of fire not equalled until the invention of the machine gun.

But after the Wars of the Roses came to an end, the high standard of English archery lapsed somewhat. It was to counter this decline that the rumbunctious game of football was outlawed in many towns and villages – so that the men would not be distracted from their militarily vital target practice. In Leicester, in 1467, an order was issued to deter men from the sport of tennis, and at around the same time in Scotland King James II promulgated a similar ban on golf. Elsewhere, it was hockey or cock-fighting that were cited as the 'dishonest games' that had to be avoided, so as not to imperil the fighting fitness of England's longbowmen.

There are places in England where the by-laws banning football have never been revoked, meaning that the beautiful game is still technically illegal. But compulsory archery practice had all but ceased everywhere in England by the time that the 16th century came to an end.

The King's Shilling
Army pay down the centuries

Considering the hardships and personal risk to which they are subjected, British soldiers are not well-paid. A present-day private soldier receives about £16,000 per year basic pay – or close to £20,000 if his year includes a six-month tour of duty in Afghanistan. By way of comparison, a traffic warden earns slightly more than private soldier – roughly £20,000 per year; a police constable with four years' experience can expect to take home £30,000. The average mean income across the UK hovers around the £23,000 mark.

It was ever thus. An Elizabethan soldier – fighting against the Spanish in the Netherlands, say – earned eightpence a day, of which three shillings (36 old pence, or 15p) were deducted each month for food. A cavalryman received half a crown a day (30 pence) but was expected to feed and maintain his own horse out of this sum. During the English Civil War and Cromwell's Protectorate, a footsoldier's pay rose to ten pence or even a shilling (12 pence) a day, but

after the Restoration it was reduced to eightpence once more. And it remained at this rate – regardless of economic fluctuations or rising prices – until the end of the American Revolutionary Wars in 1783. An infantryman fighting in the Anglo-Sudan wars of the 1880s was still only receiving a shilling a day – the same as Roundhead footsoldier might have expected to receive for his day's work at Naseby or Marston Moor.

Throughout the time that eightpence was the norm – 123 years in all – a soldier's wage was not his own to spend. His captain would hold back fourpence a day, which (in theory at least) would be paid to the innkeeper with whom the soldier was lodged. A further twopence a day was retained by the regiment for 'off-reckonings': the cost of a man's uniform and so forth. That left twopence a day – and some of that might be spent by a soldier's captain on laundry or other necessaries. During the 'War of Two Kings', when King William III sent British troops to Ireland to fight the deposed King James II, British officers were sent an order demanding that they give the troops at least some small percentage of their pay, or else be stripped of their commissions. This might have improved the ordinary soldier's finances for a short while, but the fact remains that for most of the 17th and 18th centuries, the best a British infantryman could hope for in terms of remuneration was a few pennies a week – to be spent mostly on beer and baccy.

THE CHELSEA PENSION

Though footsoldiers often were practically penniless while they served, they were likely to be even worse off once they were discharged. Large numbers of ex-soldiers – officers and men alike – were reduced to beggary or crime when they returned from the wars. Many a dashing highwayman was a cavalry officer who had been forced to make a living through robbery with menaces. It was the economic distress of old soldiers that led Charles II (at the prompting of Nell Gwynne) to found the Royal Hospital at Chelsea in 1681. The Hospital looked after men whose bodies had been broken by war or tropical diseases, and it

distributed small 'out-pensions' to other retired fighting men. This was very welcome, of course, but at the same time it was yet another drain on the pay packet of serving soldiers, each of whom had a halfpenny deducted from their pay each week to pay for the Chelsea pension.

The Songs of the Trenches
Verse and worse in the mud of Flanders

It is well known that the trenches of the First World War inspired some magnificent poetry, full of righteous anger and passion. But the works of Siegfried Sassoon, Wilfred Owen and others were little known while the fighting was going on. Most of the best war poetry was published after the guns had fallen silent, and did not begin to shape our view of the war until years or decades afterwards.

At the time, and for the vast majority of British soldiers, the experience of the war was expressed through a rather lower form of verse. These were the popular ditties of the day, which had been adapted by some anonymous wit to reflect the reality of a soldier's life. This was one that did the rounds in the early days of the war:

Tickler's jam, Tickler's jam, how
I love old Tickler's jam.
Plum and apple in a one-pound pot,
sent from Blighty in a ten-ton lot.
Every night when I'm asleep I'm
dreaming that I am
Forcing my way through the
Dardanelles with a ton of
Tickler's jam.

Tickler's jam was a regular constituent in rations in 1914 and 1915, and the slightly comical name of the firm naturally lent itself to ridicule. It was rumoured that the main ingredient of the plum jam was not plums at all, but root vegetables flavoured with fruit juice and sweetened with sugar. As for the song, in its innocence it is almost like a nursery rhyme – but for the veiled and slightly sinister reference to fighting in the last line.

As the war progressed, a rather more cynical note crept into the folk music of the front line. A recurrent theme was the folly of having volunteered in the first place.

Why did we join the army, boys?
Why did we join the army
Why did we come to France to fight?
We must be f–ing barmy!

If that song suggests that it was a terrible mistake to have enlisted, then *The Old Brigade* suggests that the volunteers had been deliberately duped by the authorities. The first two lines are a straight-faced invocation of the patriotic urge that drew hundreds of thousands of men to the recruiting offices; the second two lines, meanwhile, are a rueful and jocular admission that cowardice might have been the wiser course:

Send for the boys of the Old Brigade
To keep Old England free.
Send for me father and me mother
and me brother
But for Gawd's sake don't send for me!

A kind of grim irony, heavy as a mud-soaked boot, became the dominant tenor of soldiers' songs after the trauma of the Somme. This song, written by JP Long and Maurice Scott in 1917, quickly achieved the status of an anthem at the front. The first phrase of the first line is almost Owenesque; it is reminiscent of his 'Bent double, like old beggars under sacks…', the opening words of *Dulce et Decorum Est*. But it was the chorus, with its echoes of the Edwardian music-hall, that really caught the fighting men's imagination:

*Up to your waist in water, up to your
    eyes in slush,*
*Using the kind of language that makes
    the sergeant blush,*
*Who wouldn't join the army – that's
    what we all enquire.*
*Don't we pity the poor civilians sitting
    beside the fire.*

Oh, oh, oh, it's a lovely war!
Who wouldn't be a soldier, eh?
Oh, it's a shame to take the pay.
*As soon as reveille has gone we feel
    just as heavy as lead,*
*But we never get up till the sergeant
    brings our breakfast up to bed.*
Oh, oh, oh, it's a lovely war!

By the time the Armistice came round, the men at the front were too war-weary for that kind of cleverness. The defining song of the trenches, sung to the tune of *Auld Lang Syne*, expresses the bitterness, the exhaustion and the brain-numbing nihilism of men who had been through a hell on earth. It goes:

We're here because we're here
Because we're here because we're here
*Because we're here because we're
    here…*

… and so on *ad infinitum*, relentlessly and pointlessly as the static war itself.

The Phoney War
Total war with no fighting at all

In 1938, the former prime minister Stanley Baldwin had warned the British people that 'the bomber will always get through'. So when Britain declared war on Germany on September 3rd, 1939, everybody fully expected that the Luftwaffe would arrive that same day, and begin raining bombs on London.

Sure enough, the air raid sirens

sounded in the capital almost as soon as Neville Chamberlain finished telling the nation on the radio that 'this country is now at war with Germany' – but no German planes came, and in fact very little happened for almost a year.

People busied themselves sending their children off to the countryside to live with complete strangers – as many as one million were sent away with little more than a luggage label round their necks to identify them. The snakes in London Zoo were humanely destroyed, in case a bomb hit their enclosure and let

them loose in the city. Theatres and music halls shut their doors to the crowds. Homeowners dug large holes in their gardens and constructed 'Anderson shelters' from large sheets of corrugated iron. But after a month or two had passed without a hint of a bomb, parents began to summon their children back from their rural exile.

The main danger to life during the winter of 1939 was the precautionary 'blackout'. The number of fatalities on the roads soared because the streetlights were extinguished, and the cars were not permitted to use their headlights freely. At the end of the year, the *New Statesman* magazine wrote that the country had just lived through 'four months of the strangest war in history.'

Britain's Wars in the 20th Century
Wars and conflicts between 1900 and 1999

The Second Boer War
(1899-1902, South Africa)

The Boxer Rebellion
(1900, China)

The War of the Golden Stool
(1900, modern-day Ghana)

The Anglo-Aro war
(1901–1902, Nigeria)

The First World War
(1914–1918)

The Easter Rising
(1916, Ireland)

The Intervention in Russia
(1918–1922)

The Third Anglo-Afghan War
(1919)

The Anglo-Irish War
(1919–1921)

The Second World War
(1939–1945)

The Greek Civil War
(1941–1949)

The Malayan Emergency
(1948–1960)

The Cold War (1949-1991)

The Korean War
(1950–1953)

The Mau Mau Uprising
(1952–1960, Kenya)

The Cyprus Emergency
(1955–1959)

The Suez Crisis
(1956, Egypt)

The Dhofar Rebellion
(1962–1975, Oman)

The Konfrontasi
(1962–1966, Indonesia, Malaysia))

The Aden Emergency
(1963–1967, modern-day Yemen)

The Troubles
(1969-1998, Northern Ireland)

The Cod War
(1975–1976, off the coast of Iceland)

The Falklands War (1982)

The First Gulf War
(1990–1991, Iraq, Kuwait)

The Bosnian War
(1995–1996)

The Kosovo War (1999)

Bagpipes in Battle
Scotland's aural machine-gun

It has long been a tradition in the British army for Scottish regiments to go into battle to the sound of the bagpipes. The plangent wail of the pipes serves to stir Scots soldiers to great deeds, while at the same time striking dread and confusion into the heart of the enemy. They are a kind of musical psychological weapon.

The job of regimental piper is in many ways an unenviable one. In order to give heart to his comrades, a piper on the battlefield needs to be highly visible and audible – which naturally brings him to the attention of the enemy. He cannot carry a weapon, or defend himself at all. He is, in effect, a sitting duck, as many pipers down the centuries have found out to their cost.

One of the earliest accounts of pipers in battle concerns the Battle of Porto Novo, (present-day Parangipettai in the Indian state of Tamil Nadu), which was fought on July 1st, 1781. The bagpipe players' names are unknown, but they belonged to the 71st Regiment (1st Battalion, The Highland Light Infantry).

At least one piper was present at the Battle of Waterloo in 1815. He was called Kenneth Mackay, and he served with the 79th Cameron Highlanders. As the French cavalry were making ready to charge, he stepped out in front of his own ranks and serenaded the line of Scots soldiers as they waited, bayonets fixed, for the French to descend on them. Something similar happened during the fighting around Loos in Belgium during the First World War. Trenches occupied by the 7th Battalion of the King's Own Scottish Borderers were attacked with gas. Piper Daniel Laidlaw climbed out onto the parapet and marched up and down, above the heads of his fellows and in sight of the German guns, playing *Blue Bonnets over the Border* as he went.

The most celebrated piper of the Second World War is surely Bill

Millin, a commando of 1 Special Service Brigade (1SSB), who piped his unit onto the Normandy beaches on D-Day. His commanding officer was the eccentric Scottish aristocrat Lord Lovat, who had defied a War Office ban on taking pipers into battle, deeming it too frivolous and hazardous ('Ah, but that's the English War office,' Lovat had said to Millin. 'You and I are both Scots, so it doesn't apply.')

Millin waded ashore on Sword Beach, and played *Road to the Isles* as the shells burst and the bullets whistled all around him. He stayed with his unit as they fought their way to their objective, Pegasus Bridge, which had been captured by British paratroopers dropped into France the night before the landings. When 1SSB reached its objective, Lovat ordered Millin to play the men across the bridge, though it was still under fire from German snipers. Millin came through the fighting unscathed, and later expressed surprise to a German prisoner that he had not been hit. 'We didn't shoot at you because we assumed that you were insane,' the captured German replied.

Jenkins's Belligerent Ear
How the abuse of a sea captain caused a long-lasting war

The War of Jenkins's Ear sounds trivial, but it was a serious conflict between Britain and Spain that lasted longer than the First and Second World wars combined.

The war had its roots in the Treaty of Utrecht, under the terms of which Britain extracted an agreement from Spain to supply its colonies in the West Indies with slaves and other saleable goods. The agreement said that Spanish warships were entitled to stop British merchantmen in order to verify their cargoes.

Sometimes, it seems, the Spanish used their legal right to board British ships as a pretext for harassment and pillage. Certainly the process was not always entirely correct and courteous. In April 1731, a brig named *Rebecca* was subjected to one of these customs checks, and somehow the situation quickly turned violent. The captain of the British ship, Robert Jenkins, was tied to his own mast by a captain of the Spanish coastguard, who *'took hold of his left Ear and with his Cutlass slit it down, and then another of the Spaniards took hold of it and tore it off, but gave him the Piece of his Ear again'* (this is Jenkins speaking of his own ordeal in the third person). The Spaniard reportedly said to Jenkins: 'Go, and tell your king that I will do the same, if he dares to do the same.'

The incident occurred at a time when relations with Spain were at a low ebb, but was almost immediately forgotten. It did not become a political issue until seven years later, when Anglo–Spanish tension was again high. The mutilation of Captain Jenkins was then cited as an example of 'Spanish depredations upon British Subjects', and in March 1738 Jenkins was invited to give an account of himself to parliament. Apparently he brought his severed ear along with him – pickled in a jar – and showed it to the House. It was a theatrical gesture that seems to have had a galvanising effect on MPs, who voted in favour of seeking redress from

Spain. War was declared in October 1738, and the first naval battles of the conflict took place the following month. Hostilities did not officially end until 1748, by which time it had become subsumed in the wider War of the Austrian Succession.

It was the Victorian historian Thomas Carlyle who coined the phrase 'The War of Jenkins's Ear'. He used it jestingly in his life of Frederick the Great, published in 1858. The expression has proved more memorable than the war itself: everyone has heard of Jenkins's ear; not many people could tell you how it caused a war or when. As for Jenkins himself, he went on to serve for a while as governor of the island of St Helena. This gives him a loose connection with a whole series of wars apart from the one that bears his name, since Napoleon, in defeat and exile, lived out his days on the island that the injured Jenkins once administered for the British crown.

Fix Bayonets!
The British army's love of cold steel

For centuries the pikestaff was the default weapon of the English footsoldier. It was a fearsome thing: a pole 16 feet (about 5 metres) long, topped with a sharp point. It was monstrously unwieldy to carry, but a mass of pikemen standing six deep stuck, each one having stuck his pike at an angle in the ground, formed a kind of deadly and impenetrable defensive hedge. In attack, pikemen could deliver stabbing blows to the front ranks of the enemy well before they themselves came in range of a sword. A less cumbersome relative of the pike was the halberd, which was a mere 6 or 8 feet (about 1.5 metres) long, and was topped with combined axe and spear, so that it could wreak damage when swung in an arc, or when thrust at a foe.

The technological advance of the musket rendered the English pike and halberd obsolete in battle. There came a point when their length conferred no special advantage, because a gun – albeit unreliable and inaccurate –

could deliver death over considerably greater distances than any pole weapon. But close-quarter fighting was still a fact of war, and infantrymen needed to be equipped for it. This is what led to the introduction of the bayonet, a sword designed to be fitted to the barrel of a musket. It came from France (reputedly having been invented in the town of Bayonne) and was first used around the year 1670.

The first bayonets were simply plugged into the muzzle of the gun, like a cork in a bottle, thereby turning the firearm into a sort of short pikestaff. The two obvious drawbacks of this were that the blade was not all that securely attached and could easily drop off in the course of a fight; and that the musket could not be used for its primary purpose while the bayonet was fixed. Predictably, it took a military disaster to impress this second point on the commanders of the English army. At the Battle of Killiecrankie in 1688, two British regiments were overrun by Scottish rebels as they struggled to fix bayonets after firing a volley. When the Scots reached them, they had neither guns nor bayonets at the ready. This misfortune led to the development of the 'socket bayonet' a blade attached to a hollow ring that fitted over the muzzle of the gun, so that it could be loaded and fired with the bayonet in place. There are early English examples of these weapons dating from 1690.

Despite the obvious advantages of a weapon that could both shoot and stab, a sentimental attachment to the cut-and-thrust method of killing lingered for many decades. In the 18th century, it was not uncommon for soldiers to be ordered to advance with their bayonets fixed and their muskets unloaded (though in some instances this was to prevent an accidental discharge that would give away an ambush party). There seems to have been a feeling that guns alone made battle just too easy for the troops. At the Battle of Sobraon in 1846, in the course of the First Sikh War, General Sir Hugh Gough expressed himself delighted that his men's ammunition was running out. 'Thank God,' he said. 'Then I'll be at them with the bayonet.'

The use of the bayonet remained an integral part of training for officers and men in both the world wars, and into the era of National Service. 'In my training as a young officer I received much instruction on how to kill my enemy with a bayonet fixed to a rifle,' recalled General Montgomery, speaking of his experiences in the First World War. I knew all about the various movement – right parry, left parry, forward lunge. I had been taught how to put the left foot on the corpse and extract the bayonet, giving at the same time a loud grunt. I had been considered good on the bayonet-fighting course against sacks filled with straw…' The poet Siegfried Sassoon recalled being taught the art of the bayonet by a major, ably assisted by a sergeant who 'had been trained to such a pitch of frightfulness that at a moment's warning he could divest himself of all semblance of humanity. When told to put on a "killing face" he did so, combining it with an ultra-vindictive attitude. Man, it seemed, had been created to jab the life out of Germans.'

In the world wars, one of the functions of the bayonet was to 'instil fear into the opponent'. That is to say, its effect was as much psychological as tactical, since the prospect of being run through by a snarling, red-faced enemy was somehow so much more terrifying than being struck by an anonymous bullet. Bayonet injuries were cruel, particularly since British soldiers were trained to 'thrust the bayonet home, then give it a sharp twist to the left, thus making the wound fatal'. Perhaps the shock-and-awe value of the bayonet is what made those 19th-century generals so enamoured of it.

Even now, the bayonet has its military uses. Strangely, many of the modern instances of bayonet use seem to feature Scottish soldiers and regiments. At the Battle of Tumbledown Mount, during the Falklands War, a night-time bayonet charge by elements of the Scots Guards helped drive the Argentinian defenders off the mountaintop. In Iraq in 2004, a patrol of the Argyll and Sutherland Highlanders ran 200 metres across open ground to engage insurgents with bayonets. The incident is known as the Battle of Danny Boy, after the name of the checkpoint where it took place.

And in 2009, Lieutenant James

Adamson of the Royal Regiment of Scotland was awarded the Military Cross for a single-handed attack with fixed bayonet, directed at a Taliban machine-gunner. 'I either wasted vital seconds changing the magazine on my rifle or went over the top and did it more quickly with the bayonet,' he said afterwards. 'I took the second option. There was no inner monologue; I was just reacting in the way that I was trained. He was alive when it went in, he wasn't alive when it came out. It was that simple.'

A Black Week in Boer Country
Three military disasters in South Africa

Britsh commanders at the start of the Boer War had little idea about how to tackle their enemy. They saw the Boers as amateurs, mere ragtag bands of Dutch farmers who would stand no chance against the might of the British Empire. This was massively to underestimate the Boers: they were organised; they were determined to defend their country; they could move swiftly and they had all grown up with rifles in their hands. 'The Boers can shoot,' said Paul Kruger, President of the Transvaal, 'And that is everything.'

The ill-founded and ill-disguised contempt of the British generals for the Boers was dramatically exposed during one catastrophic week in December 1899, when three separate British columns were engaged and defeated by the Boers. The first incident occurred at Stormberg. A 3,000-strong force under General Sir William Gatacre (known to his men as Back-Acher because of the heavy packs he made them carry) was ambushed by Boer pickets who were entrenched high on a *kopje* – a small hill – and armed with Mausers, machine guns and light artillery. Some of the British infantrymen rushed forward, but found themselves pinned down by 'friendly fire' coming from the gunners behind them. Ninety British soldiers were killed, and when Gatacre ordered a retreat, 600 of the men who had stormed the hill were left behind, to be captured by the Boers.

The Battle of Magersfontein took place next day, far to the north. The British column was marching on Kimberley to relieve the Boer siege of the town. The commander,

General Methuen, knew that the Boers were waiting for his arrival, but he failed to reconnoitre thoroughly. He assumed that the Boers were occupying the high ground as usual, and on the afternoon of December 10th he ordered his artillery to bombard the ridge ahead of him. In fact the Boers were dug in, invisibly, in trenches at the foot of the hills, and were left untouched by the thorough shelling.

Methuen ordered the Highland Brigade to advance under cover of darkness. In the teeming rain, the 2nd Black Watch, the 1st Highland Light Infantry, the 2nd Seaforth Highlanders and the 1st Argyll and Sutherland Highlanders crept up towards the Magersfontein Hills. They advanced in close order so as not to lose each other in inky night: 3,500 men in kilts, so tightly formed up that they rubbed shoulders as they walked. The Highland Brigade stopped as dawn broke, not realising that the Boers were entrenched less than 400 yards ahead of them. They were about to deploy into a more open attack formation when the Boers began to fire from their sunken hiding places.

700 Scotsmen were killed in the first five minutes of the engagement, and the rest of the brigade was pinned down helplessly for the rest of the day. More than 900 British soldiers died in the course of the battle – most of that balance of 200 men being shot down while trying to retreat.

A third column, meanwhile, was on its way to relieve the town of Ladysmith. On December 15th, the British force advanced towards the village of Colenso, which sat on the banks of the Tugela River, some miles south of Ladysmith. An inexperienced native guide led the main force to a ford in a loop of the river that happened to be well within range of the Boer guns.

Though the Boers had intended to engage the British after they had made the crossing, and had the river behind them, the crowd of soldiery crammed into the curl of the river was too much of a gift to refuse. They poured fire into the British ranks, killing 500 men. Meanwhile the British artillery had advanced too close to the Boer lines, and the gunners came under heavy fire. They had to abandon their guns and take cover in a dry river bed. All in all ten guns were lost, and more than a thousand men killed. The British column withdrew. It took another two and a half months, and yet another disastrous encounter at Spion Kop in January 1900, to break through the Boer lines and finally relieve Ladysmith.

The three defeats at Stormberg, Magersfontein and Colenso came to be known collectively as 'Black Week'. They were deeply disheartening for the British rank-and-file. One anonymous member of the Black Watch, a man who had fought at Magersfontein, wrote a poem that in its bitterness prefigures the disillusion of the men who volunteered for the trenches in the First World War:

> Such was the day for our regiment,
> Dread the revenge we will take
> Dearly we paid for the blunder
> A drawing-room General's mistake.
>
> Why weren't we told of the trenches?
> Why weren't we told of the wire?
> Why were we marched up in column,
> May Tommy Atkins enquire…

UP, UP AND AWAY

The British used hot-air balloons for scouting purposes in the Boer War. It was a rather hazardous way to conduct aerial reconnaissance considering that the Boers were such fine shots, and the Boers always did their best to bring them down. But the British military balloonists were generally canny enough to keep out of range. The Boers considered ballooning a rather unsporting tactic on the part of the British. 'It is amusing to hear the talk of some of our Burghers,' wrote one Boer fighter, 'such as "Do you call this fair play, that damnable big round thing, spying our positions?" We would not be so mean as to do a thing like this.'

Blood, Toil, Tears and Sweat
Churchill's wartime speeches

Winston Churchill's speeches are one of the great cultural legacies of the Second World War – no less enduring and valuable, in their way, than the magnificent body of poetry that came out of the First World War. The writer Vita Sackville-West said of Churchill's oratory, having just listened to one of his declamations on the BBC: 'I think that one of the reasons why one is so stirred by his Elizabethan phrases is that one feels the whole massive backing of power and resolve behind them, like a great fortress.'

The American reporter Ed Murrow, who was based in London in the early years of the war, had a similar thought. He said that Churchill 'mobilised the English language and sent it into battle'. Churchill himself was well aware of the power of his words. He knew that his job was to express the determination of the British people to defeat Nazism, and at the same time to strengthen and bolster that

determination. 'They had the lion's heart,' he said modestly after the war's end. 'I had the luck to be called upon to give the roar.'

Here are some of Churchill's most memorable lines, all of them spoken in the sternest days of the war, when the United Kingdom stood alone against an enemy that had occupied all of Europe.

You ask, what is our policy? I will say: It is to wage war, by sea, land and air, with all our might and with all the strength that God can give us. To wage war against a monstrous tyranny, never surpassed in the dark, lamentable catalogue of human crime. That is our policy. You ask: what is our aim? I can answer in one word: Victory. Victory at all costs, victory in spite of all terror, victory, however long and hard the road may be.

May 1940

*

I have nothing to offer but blood, toil, tears and sweat.

May 1940

*

The whole might and fury of the enemy must very soon be turned upon us. Hitler knows that he will have to break us in this island or lose the war. If we can stand up to him, all Europe may be free and the life of the world may move forward into broad, sunlit uplands. But if we fail, then the whole world, including the United States, including all that we have known and cared for, will sink into the abyss of a new Dark Age made more sinister, and perhaps more protracted, by the lights of perverted science. Let us therefore brace ourselves to our duties and so bear ourselves that, if the British Empire and its Commonwealth last for a thousand years, men will say: this was their finest hour.

June 1940

★

We shall go on to the end, we shall fight in France, we shall fight on the seas and oceans, we shall fight with growing confidence and growing strength in the air, we shall defend our Island, whatever the cost may be, we shall fight on the beaches, we shall fight on the landing grounds, we shall fight in the fields and in the streets, we shall fight in the hills; we shall never surrender.

June 1940

★

The gratitude of every home in our island, in our Empire, and indeed throughout the world except in the abodes of the guilty goes out to the British airmen who, undaunted by odds, unweakened by their constant challenge and mortal danger, are turning the tide of world war by their prowess and their devotion. Never in the field of human conflict was so much owed by so many to so few.

August 1940

★

This is the lesson: never give in. Never give in, never, never, never, never; in nothing, great or small, large or petty. Never give in except to convictions of honour and good sense. Never yield to force; never yield to the apparently overwhelming might of the enemy.

October 1941

★

Slaves of War
The soldiers bought at market

In the first Kandy War, fought in Ceylon (modern-day Sri Lanka) in 1803, so large a part of the British forces was laid low by sickness that the British Army was forced to buy reinforcements in the form of African slaves.

These unfortunate recruits were purchased at markets in Mozambique for the price of £37 a head, including freight and agents' fees. They were shipped to Ceylon, put in uniform, and deployed as garrison troops in forts such as the one at Trincomalee on the eastern coast of the island. Though morally abhorrent, the enforced enrolment of African slaves made sound military sense. The African soldiers coped much better with the climate than white European soldiers – and the mere sight of them terrified the Ceylonese rebels against whom Britain was fighting.

The Number of the Few
Some Battle of Britain statistics

The deathless heroism of its pilots apart, the RAF had certain key advantages in the Battle of Britain. Production of aircraft in Britain was greater in the crucial months than in Germany. Britain also had the technological advantage of radar. Reichsmarschall Göring, though he had been an ace pilot during the First World War, was not a good tactician

and did not allow his pilots sufficient latitude: they were too closely tied to a bomber-escort role. The pilots were the most valuable resource on both sides, and this too worked in favour of the RAF. Crucially, a German pilot who was shot down over Britain was out of the game for the rest of the war because he immediately became a prisoner, whereas an RAF pilot who bailed out safely would very likely go on to fight another day. Here are some telling statistics from the battle:

RAF pilots who took part	2,367
Non-British RAF pilots	489
RAF pilots killed in action	446
RAF pilots killed, missing, captured or wounded	903
Number of Hurricanes lost in battle	601
Number of Spitfires lost in battle	357
Total number of aircraft lost by RAF	1,087
Total number of aircraft lost by Luftwaffe	1,562

THE LAST OF THE RED COATS

Most regiments of the British army routinely wore red coats well into the 19th century. Its distinctive colour was a liability in wars against guerillas such as the Boers or America's revolutionaries. These skilled hunters and sharpshooters, fighting in their own familiar country, had no trouble spotting their conspicuously attired enemy, and could pretty much pick off individuals at will. In India, soldiers wore khaki for some purposes, but the

War Office in London was slow to abandon the traditional red costume altogether. The last campaign in which British soldiers went into battle wearing red was General Gordon's Khartoum expedition of 1884. Scarlet jackets are still worn on ceremonial occasions by the regiments of the Life Guards and the Foot Guards.

Chums on the Somme
The pals' battalions

In the first recruitment drive of 1914, young men were encouraged to join up with their friends and colleagues. They were told that they would be able to serve alongside the people that they knew and grew up with, rather than be distributed randomly to different regiments. This promise provided a huge boost to the numbers queueing up to enlist, and gave rise to the peculiar phenomenon known as 'pals' battalions', units made up almost entirely of men from the same factory, the same streets, the same social club or profession.

Very often the provenance of the 'pals' was unofficially incorporated into their regimental names. The 11th

East Lancashire Regiment was known as 'The Accrington Pals'; the 10th Lincolns were 'The Grimsby Chums'. There was a 'Tramways Battalion' raised from transport workers in Glasgow, and a miners battalion – the 12th Kings Own Yorkshire Light Infantry. Though many of the pals' battalions were made up of working-class volunteers from the north of the country, the pals idea extended to other locations and other classes. A stockbrokers' battalion – consisting of white-collar workers from the City of London – was to be found in the ranks of the Royal Fusiliers. There was also a footballers' battalion in the Middlesex Regiment, its recruits all drawn from the side then known as Clapton Orient (now Leyton Orient). In Scotland, every player in the first and the reserve team of Heart of Midlothian Football Club joined up together, along with a sizeable contingent of the club's supporters. Then there were farmers' battalions, artists' battalions and boxers' battalions. There were even 'bantam battalions', comprising men who were not boxers, but happened to be less than 5 feet 3 inches (160 centimetres) tall – that is below what had previously been considered the minimum height for a British soldier.

The pals' battalions were in training in Britain throughout 1915, but most of them made it to France in time for the Battle of the Somme, on July 1st, 1916. Here, a great many of the pals died together. In some cases, all the young men of a village or a factory were annihilated in the first attack on the German lines. The Chorley Pals lost 93 men out of 175. Of the 700 Accrington Pals, 585 were killed or wounded within half an hour of climbing out of their trenches. One of their officers later wrote of the men of Accrington: 'Those Lancashire lads went over smoking and joking, as calmly as though going to their dinner.'

COFFIN COUNT
At the outbreak of the Second World War, the British government ordered a million coffins to be stockpiled – for the victims of air raids. In the event, 60,000 Britons were killed by German bombing raids over the course of the war.

Gallant She-Soldiers
*Fighting women of the
18th century*

There is a long and rather glorious tradition of British women passing themselves off as men in order to enlist in the army and fight in wars. It is a practice that seems to have been particularly prevalent in the 18th century.

Among the outstanding women soldiers to have served in the British army was Hannah Snell. She was an extraordinarily tough and resourceful soldier. She was born in Worcester in 1723, married young, and soon found that married life was not to her liking. To escape her husband, she borrowed a suit of clothes from her brother-in-law and also took his name – James Gray. She made her way to Carlisle where, in 1745, she enlisted in a regiment of foot. Here she committed some offence, and was sentenced to 500 lashes. She underwent the punishment – apparently without her sex being discovered in the process – then deserted that regiment and went to Portsmouth, where she joined a battalion of marines about to set sail for India. She took part in the siege of Pondicherry in 1748, where she received 12 wounds in her upper legs. She treated herself so as to preserve her secret, going so far as to 'thrust in both her finger and her thumb' to remove a musket ball from a wound in her thigh.

Her short but admirable career in the army ended in 1750, and she returned to England with her alias intact. When she made her story known, she was awarded a pension by the Duke of Cumberland (the so-called Butcher of Culloden). She used the money to open a pub, which she called The Widow in Masquerade.

The story of Mother Ross is even more remarkable – and better known, because her biography was written up by Daniel Defoe. Her real name was Kit Cavanagh, and she joined the army in 1693 to find her husband, Richard Walsh, who had apparently been press-ganged after getting blind-drunk in a Dublin tavern. She left her children with her mother, then 'I cut off my hair, and dressed me in a suit of my husband's having first had the precaution to quilt the waistcoat, to preserve my breasts from hurt, which were not large enough to betray my sex, and putting on the wig and hat I had prepared, I went out and bought me a silver-hilted sword'. In this disguise, she presented herself to a recruiting ensign and 'offered my service to go against the French, being desirous to show my zeal for his majesty King William. The hopes of soon meeting my husband added a sprightliness to my looks, which made the officer say I was a clever brisk

young fellow. He gave me a guinea enlisting money, and a crown to drink the king's health, and ordered me to be enrolled, having told him my name was Christopher Walsh.'

Now her adventures really began. As infantryman Walsh, she fought at the Battle of Landen, where she was wounded and captured. She was exchanged in 1694 and returned to her regiment. So deeply had she immersed herself in her disguise that she somehow became involved in a dispute with a sergeant from her company over the affections of a woman. The love-rivals fought a duel with swords in the course of which Mrs Walsh killed the sergeant.

She was discharged from the regiment soon after, but promptly re-enlisted with the Scots Greys. By this time she had clearly mastered her disguise. She had even learned to urinate standing up, using a contraption consisting of 'a silver tube and leather straps'. But it must have been a worry to her that she was known to her comrades-in-arms as the 'pretty dragoon'.

Mrs Walsh kept up her pretence for well over a decade. She was wounded again at the Battle of Schellenberg (1704), and took part in the Battle of Blenheim later the same year. It was after Blenheim that she finally caught up with her husband, who happened to be importuning a Dutch woman in the moment that she found him. This naturally put Mr Walsh at a disadvantage, and he agreed to keep his wife's secret. They both said that they were brothers to explain away the fact that they had the same surname.

Mrs Walsh's military career came to an end at the Battle of Ramillies, where she was wounded again. 'An unlucky shell struck the back part of my head and fractured my skull. Though I suffered great torture by this wound, yet the discovery it caused of my sex in the fixing of my dressing, by which the surgeons saw my breasts, was a greater grief to me. No sooner had they made this discovery but that they acquainted Brigadier Preston that his pretty dragoon was in fact a woman. He was very loath to believe it, and did me the honour to say he had always looked upon me as the best man he had.'

Mrs Walsh – Mother Ross, as she now became known – stayed on with the army as a sutler. But she could not resist the call of battle: at the Siege of Ath she took up a gun and was again wounded by a musket ball that struck her in the face. She later retired on a pension of a shilling a day; and when she died in 1739, she was buried with full military honours in a cemetery belonging to the Chelsea Hospital.

Nothing But a Miracle
The Dunkirk evacuation

In May 1940, as France fell to the invading Germans, the British Expeditionary Force was forced back towards the French coast. It looked like the entire British army in France would be lost, along with the remnants of the French army. 'Nothing but a miracle can save the BEF now,' wrote General Alan Brooke on May 23rd. And the miracle came – or the glimmer of one – the next day. Hitler suddenly became anxious that his tanks were too exposed in the open canal-riven flatlands, and ordered them to halt for two days. This brief respite allowed a third of a million soldiers to converge on the port of Dunkirk.

Frantic preparations were by now being made to evacuate as many men as possible before the Germans closed in. The Admiralty was assembling every available ship and sending it over the Channel to carry back the defeated BEF. But the Royal Navy ships were not alone: they were joined by ferries, river boats, pleasure steamers, and small cabin cruisers manned by their civilian owners. This motley armada converged on Dunkirk, and every vessel took back as many men as it could hold. Many of the ships made repeated trips, their crewmen going without rest or food for days on end. On the night of May 26th, 8,000 men were evacuated; on May 28th, 19,000; on May 31st, 68,000. A total of 340,000 men were saved by the time the evacuation ended on June 4th – more than 100,000 of them Frenchmen.

As for the soldiers at Dunkirk, they queued for days, waiting for their turn to be ferried across the water. It was a terrible ordeal, made infinitely worse by the constant strafing of the beaches by Luftwaffe fighter planes. Many

soldiers were killed as they waited to be rescued. 'The picture will always remain sharp-etched in my memory,' wrote one seaman who was there. 'The lines of men wearily and sleepily staggering across the beach from the dunes to the shallows, falling into little boats, great columns of men thrust out into the water among bomb and shell splashes. As the front ranks were dragged aboard the boats the rear ranks moved up, from ankle-deep to knee-deep, from knee-deep to waist-deep, until they came to shoulder depth and took their turn. The little boats listed drunkenly with the weight of the men…'

The Maid of Orleans
Joan of Arc and her war against the English

The most famous female soldier in history was not an Englishwoman, but an enemy of England. Joan of Arc was born in the Lorraine region of France in around 1412, three years before the Battle of Agincourt. Her family were prosperous farmers, uprooted by the war that England brought

to her native country. At about the age of 12, she began to have visions of saints Michael, Margaret and Catherine 'accompanied by many angels from heaven'. The saints told her that she was to bring the dauphin – the heir to the French throne – to Rheims for his coronation.

At about the age of 16 she managed to gain an audience with the dauphin. Something about her fervour impressed him, or perhaps he was just clutching at straws because the military situation was so desperate.

At any rate, Joan persuaded the dauphin to equip her for battle and place her at the head of his army. She arrived at the Siege of Orléans, where by sheer force of personality she transformed a despondent stalemate into an aggressive and ultimately victorious onslaught. Under her banner, the demoralised French defenders of Orléans mounted a series of raids that put the English to flight. The same feat was accomplished at other cities throughout the Loire.

How exactly Joan made such a difference is still a subject of debate and controversy. Most authorities doubt that she was a great general. She was however possessed of a mystical conviction that it was her destiny to drive the English from France. She had the military leader's gift of being able to transmit her own courage and confidence to the soldiers under her command. It was this inspirational quality that made her a formidable enemy. She was a prophetess in shining armour, a schoolgirl Henry V, and she turned the tide of the Hundred Years War in France's favour. Just over two months after Orléans, the dauphin arrived in

Rheims, and was crowned Charles VII – exactly as Joan had foretold.

But the saintly voices that spoke to her did not always give her sound military advice. She now promised that the armies of France would be able to take Paris, then occupied by England's allies, the Burgundians. The campaign failed, and many French knights began to resent her influence over Charles. When she was captured by the Burgundians at Compiègne, parts of her own army were as pleased as her enemies. The Burgundians sold her to the English, who put her on trial for heresy. She was questioned closely about her visions, and also about her apparently suspicious preference for male attire. She was convicted, and burned at the stake. She was 19 years old at the time of her terrible death.

Naming of Parts
Poets of the Second World War

It is sometimes wondered why the First World War produced so many fine poets, while the Second World War failed to do so. Was there something about the ghastly and unforeseen novelty of trench warfare that was a fit subject for poetic expression – like Dante's *Inferno* made real? Was it that, come 1939, the horror of war was too workaday, altogether too prosaic, to be explored in lyrical form?

Or perhaps it was that the second war lacked the ambivalence of the

first? In the Great War there was the suspicion among thoughtful soldiers that the whole thing was a dreadful absurdity, that the Germans in the opposing trenches were not enemies, but fellow victims. In the war against Hitler there was none of that doubt about the cause – and doubt of one kind or another is often the wellspring of literary creativity. Who knows. But one answer to the conundrum may be that the premise is wrong: there were in fact many fine poets writing about their experiences in the war against Nazi Germany. Perhaps none of them speak in the same way or with quite the same tragic eloquence as Wilfred Owen, but he was a rare genius fighting in a static war: for all the horrors, there was time to sit down and write.

One of the best-known poems of the Second World War is Henry Reed's *Naming of Parts*. With exquisite irony, it contrasts barrack-ground drill with the serene beauty of nature:

> …*And this is the piling swivel,*
> *Which in your case you have not got.*
> *The branches*
> *Hold in the gardens their silent,*

> *eloquent gestures,*
> *Which in our case we have not got.*

There is a wry humour in those words, a nonchalance, and that is one of the features of the poetry of the Second World War – maybe because the combatants were, on the whole, older and wiser than their fathers had been in their war. The poet TW Ramsey described the bombing of British cities in these allusive terms:

> *The draggled flowers and the broken vases,*
> *And Churchill shouting insults at the Nazis.*

Earlier, Ramsey made this modest comment about his role fighting with the Eighth Army in North Africa:

> *The papers called us heroes, but we knew*
> *A hero is a visionary being,*
> *Uncomfortable to live with probably, –*
> *In Greece perhaps you might find one or two.*

Some of the finest poetry of the war was written by RAF men –

perhaps because poets and pilots alike tend to be sensitive, well-educated, middle-class boys. The most famous verse by an RAF flyer is John Gillespie Magee's *High Flight*. He was a British-American Spitfire pilot, and his experience of climbing high in that wonderful aircraft led him to write a sonnet that begins:

> *Oh! I have slipped the surly bonds*
>   *of Earth*
> *And danced the skies on laughter-*
>   *silvered wings;*
> *Sunward I've climbed and joined the*
>   *tumbling mirth of sun-split clouds…*

In 1941, when Magee penned those lines, he was 19 and newly qualified. He still only 19 when, later that year, he was killed in a midair collision. The poem was discovered in his effects on the day of his death. Forty-five years later, in 1986, President Ronald Reagan quoted from it in his eulogy to the Americans who died in the Challenger space shuttle – and since then *High Flight* (most especially its last line 'I've… put out my hand and touched the face of God..') has been a kind of motto for

astronauts as well as aviators.

There is one short elegiac verse that bridges both world wars, because it was coined in the First, and is often used as an epitaph for those who fell in the Second. The lines were written in 1916 by a man named John Maxwell Edmonds, and were first inscribed on the war memorial to the 2nd Division at Kohima (1,420 men are buried here, in a cemetery which is on the site of a bloody battle against the Japanese in 1944). The lines read:

> *When you go home*
> *Tell them of us and say*
> *For your tomorrow*
> *We gave our today.*

Not The Hundred Years War
Changing fortunes over a century and more

The Hundred Years War between England and France was not one war but several – and it did not last 100 years, but 118. It is generally held to have begun in 1337, with the French attack on the English-held Duchy of Guyenne, and to have ended in 1453, when the English were driven from Bordeaux. At the beginning of the war the English longbow was the dominant weapon; by its end the French cannon was in the ascendent.

For four generations of English men, the war with France was one route to adventure, to fame and – most especially – to fortune. Younger sons of the nobility could make a tidy sum by serving as mercenaries; others grew rich from plunder.

Many of the rank-and-file soldiers in the English armies were raised by 'indenture', meaning that the king hired local commissioners to raise a certain number of troops who were contracted to serve for a fixed period of time. The commissioners were supposed to select the best fighters, or at least the young men with the most potential to be good soldiers. In practice, their first port of call was usually the local gaol or dungeon. It has been estimated that every eighth soldier in the army of Edward III was a convicted murderer, a man hoping to receive a 'charter of pardon' by killing again – only this time in the name of the king.

Hobart's Funnies
The crazy but deadly tanks of D-Day

The preparations for D-Day, the allied invasion of France in 1944, were swathed in all kinds of secrecy. There were the big secrets, such as the landing zone for the proposed invasion, but there were also hundreds of smaller secrets and sleights of hand – newfangled weapons and tactics, fictional armies and pretend aircraft intended to confuse German intelligence, coded instructions to the French resistance to blow up railway lines on the day, and so hamper the movement of German troops...

But of all the hush-hush D-Day projects, the 79th (Experimental) Tank Brigade was perhaps the most bizarre. The unit was the brainchild of Major-General Percy Cleghorn Stanley Hobart. He was a veteran of the First World War and a professional soldier. In the 1920s, he transferred from the Royal Engineers to the Royal Tanks Corps, because he foresaw that the tank would be the crucial weapon in the next conflict. Between the wars he did much to develop the thinking about the tactical use of tanks, but his work was largely ignored by the military authorities. The War Office at the time was dominated by cavalry offices, who were deeply suspicious of the mobile armour. Moreover, Hobart himself was an irascible and somewhat tactless individual – rather like his brother-in-law General Montgomery – and he offended or alienated many

of the high-ranking officers who might have championed his ideas. By the time the Second World War broke out, Hobart had been eased into retirement.

In 1940, Hobart found himself the subject of a newspaper article lamenting the fact that so much military expertise was being wasted. The piece pointed out that Hobart

– a theorist and strategist of immense talent – was presently serving as a lance-corporal in the Home Guard. Winston Churchill saw the paper, and summoned Hobart to lunch. Hobart came away with his old rank back, command of a tank regiment, and the prime minister's blessing for any experiment he chose to carry out.

Hobart put his mind to adapting tanks for the task of punching through Hitler's Atlantic wall, the solid concrete defences that defended the coast of France. The strange hybrid tanks that he developed became known as 'Hobart's Funnies'. Certainly he or his men gave them peculiar names – but when it came to sending them into the fray on D-Day they turned out to be deadly serious in every way.

Among Hobart's innovations was the amphibious 'Double Duplex' tank. It had canvas skirts that meant it could float like a ship until it reached land, at which point the skirts fell away and the tank could begin blasting away at pillboxes. It was an elegant way of addressing one of the problems with tanks as part of a seaborne invasion force: they were sitting ducks during the slow and cumbersome process of debarkation from a stationary landing craft.

Then there was the Crocodile, a terrifying flame-throwing tank. And there was the Crab, a tank fitted with a spinning drum to which were attached long weighted chains. The chains thrashed the ground ahead of the tank setting off any landmines as it went, so that troops could follow safely in its wake.

There was the 'funny' known as the Flying Dustbin, which carried a huge mortar like an oil drum on its turret instead of a gun. At short range, it could blast a hole in a defensive concrete wall. A similar function was performed by the 'Double Onion' – a tank carrying two demolition charges on a metal frame. The tank simply drove up to the enemy defences, dropped the frame against the wall, retired to a safe distance and detonated it. The one-charge version of the same thing was not called, as you might expect, the Single Onion, but a 'Carrot'.

Hobart also had in his menagerie a tank that carried a box-girder bridge that could be laid across anti-tank traps or shell holes; and the strange vehicle called a Bobbin that laid thick matting as it advanced, and so made an instant roadway over soft ground for following trucks.

Hobart had other ideas that seemed no less outlandish at the time, but now look like common sense. In the teeth of opposition from his detractors at the War Office, he insisted that tanks be equipped with radios, so that the commanders could communicate and coordinate in the same way as RAF pilots in flight; and he suggested that advancing tanks should be supported with airdrops of fuel and other necessities so that their progress need not be slowed by logistical problems – which is now entirely standard practice.

Hobart was, in short, a first-class military genius – though it took as fine a judge of character as Winston Churchill to recognise it. General Eisenhower, supreme commander of Allied forces on D-Day, saw it too. He later wrote that: 'Apart from the factor of tactical surprise, the comparatively light casualties which we sustained on all beaches, except Omaha, were in large measure due to the success of the novel mechanical contrivances which we employed, and to the staggering moral and material effect of the mass of armour landed in the leading waves of the assault. It is doubtful if the assault forces could have firmly established themselves without the help of these weapons.'

GASCONS AND PORTINGALS

The army that Henry VIII took to France in 1544 was at the time the largest force under English command ever to set foot on the Continent. But England lacked many of the specialists that a besieging army required – heavy cavalry, skilled musketeers – and as a result as many as one in four of Henry's men were foreigners. It was (according to one disapproving Welsh man-at-arms) a truly international force: 'brutish soldiers from all nations under the sun – Welsh, English, Cornish, Irish, Manx, Scots, Spaniards, Gascons, Portingals, Italians, Albanians, Greeks, Turks. Almains, Germans, Burgundians, Flemings… come there to have a good time under the king of England, who was too hospitable to foreigners.'

The Last Hour of the Great War
Death and sadness on Armistice Day, November 11, 1918

The First World War came to a conclusion at the 11th hour of the 11th day of the 11th month, 1918. In the trenches, the war was waged to the bitter end – and, in certain parts of the line – even after the bitter end. One English captain recorded in his diary: 'At 11.15 it was found necessary to end the days of a Hun machine-gunner on our front who would keep on shooting. The armistice was already in force, but there was no alternative. Perhaps his watch was wrong, but he was probably the last German killed in the war – a most unlucky individual!'

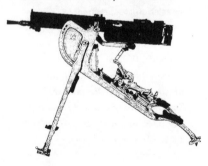

Near Mons, meanwhile, it was noted that a German gunner was still shooting at 10.59. That soldier sensibly desisted on the stroke of 11. He then stood up, removed his pickelhaube helmet, bowed to watching Englishmen, and walked off in the direction of Germany. That might have brought a smile to the lips of some weary soldiers, but generally there was no cheering, no celebrations at all, when at last the guns fell silent.

THE YEAR OF VICTORIES
1759 was a 'year of victories' for Britain. Her army fought and won wars in various corners of the globe. A small force under Lieutenant-Colonel Worge launched a sea-borne attack against the French slave station on the island of Gorée (off the coast of present-day Senegal). The bombardment of the naval guns caused havoc among the French garrison, which surrendered at negligible cost. This battle opened the way to the capture of many French possessions in West Africa. In the Caribbean, Colonel John Barrington captured the island of Guadeloupe, and in India Robert Clive won the Battle of

Plassey. In August a German-British alliance defeated the French at the Battle of Minden in Westphalia. The British regiments fought with wild roses in their hats, having picked them from gardens as they marched through the German countryside. An ambiguously worded order sent six British infantry regiments, along with three Hanoverian ones, marching straight towards the French cavalry (a strange premonition of the Charge of the Light Brigade, then a century in the future). The British soldiers ought to have been trampled and cut to pieces, but instead they smashed their way through the French line. Marshall Contades, the French commander, said after the battle that 'I never thought to see a single line of infantry break through three lines of cavalry ranked in order of battle and tumble them to ruin.'

Wolfe's victory at Quebec came the following month, and it was the culmination of a military **annus mirabilis** *for Britain.*

Richard, the Cruel Crusader
Barbarity and mass murder in the Third Crusade

Richard Coeur-de-Lion, the crusader king, is often portrayed as a model of Anglo-Norman chivalry. But as a war leader he was as harsh and brutal, a kind of medieval Stalin. He was at his most barbarous during the wars of the Third Crusade, launched to win back Jerusalem from Saladin, Sultan of Egypt. Richard had taken the city of Acre along with a large number of prisoners. He made an offer to Saladin: he would hand over his Muslim captives in exchange for the True Cross (then in Saladin's possession), plus a large ransom and any Christian prisoners that Saladin's army was holding.

Saladin played for time, knowing that he had reinforcements on the way. His plan was to make a surprise assault on Richard's army once the fresh troops arrived. But Richard's patience ran out first. On August 20th, 1191, he gave orders for the 3,000 prisoners – men, women and children – to be bound and led out to a hill called Ayyadieh, a mile or two from Acre. He chose this spot because it was clearly visible from Saladin's headquarters, on the other side of the valley. In full view of Saladin's army, every one of the captives was put to death with mallets and axes.

Saladin's men were outraged. They rushed across the valley towards the crusader army, hoping to save a few captives or, at least, exact some revenge. But they were held off, and could not reach Ayyadieh. As they attacked, some of the English infantrymen were engaged in cutting open the bodies of their victims, as they believed that some of them had swallowed gold coins to hide them from their captives.

After the massacre and the failed attack on their ranks, Richard's army retired to the city in good order, leaving their enemy to mourn and to bury the dead.

Britain's Wars since the Millennium
Armed conflict involving British forces in the 21st century

When the Cold War ended in the early 1990s there was much talk of a 'peace dividend'. The optimistic hope was that the money and resources previously invested in war and preparations for war might now become available for other, more pacific projects. Sadly, that did not come to pass. Here is a list of the wars in which Britain has engaged so far this century.

Sierra Leone civil war (2000)
Yugoslav wars (ended 2001)
War in Afghanistan (2001–2014)
War On Terror (2001–present)
The Iraqi War and Insurgency (2003-2011)
The Libyan Civil War (2011)
Military intervention against the Islamic State of Iraq and the Levant (2014–present)
Iraqi Civil War (2014–present)
War in Afghanistan (2015–present)
Mosul offensive (2015)
Mosul offensive (2016)
Battle of Mosul (2016-2017)

INDEX

Amazing and Extraordinary Facts: London At War
Stephen Halliday
ISBN: 978-1-910821-084

Amazing and Extraordinary Facts Series: Churchill
Joseph Piercy
ISBN: 978-1 -910821-077

Amazing and Extraordinary
Facts Series: Kings & Queens
Malcolm Day
ISBN: 978-1 -910821-213

Amazing and Extraordinary
Facts Series: J.R.R. Tolkien
Colin Duriez
ISBN: 978-1 -910821-268

For more great books visit our website at **www.rydonpublishing.co.uk**

Acknowledgments

I'd like to thank my sister-in-law Alison Bastable, to whom this book is dedicated, for all her brilliant and cheerful help with the research. Thank you, Kim Davies, for reading the manuscript and proofs, and righting many wrongs. I am also very grateful to Tim Ward for granting such generous access to the holdings of the Prince Consort's Army Library in Aldershot.

Picture credits

p13 Dave Hitchborne, p14 Steve Webster, p20 Matthew G. Bisanz, p25 .Sébastien Bertrand, p39 Nxn0405ch1, p51 Greg L, p73 www.adamsguns.com, p82 Walther Dobbertin, p103 ceridwen